Text

 Mèsy
Bartoli

Barbara
Latini

Illustrations

 Monica
Verdiani

D1219792

Explore and discover

Siena

A guidebook
to the city
especially for children

Betti
EDITRICE

With the support and cooperation of

The Ministry of Culture
Sponsorship of the Superintendence of Artistic Works
and the historians of the provinces of Siena and Grosseto

The Provincial Administration of Siena
- The Office of Tourism
- The Office of Culture

COMUNE DI SIENA

SIENA APT
AGENZIA PER IL TURISMO

SIENA VIVA
Servizi per i Beni
Culturali ed il Turismo

This guidebook is dedicated to Alice, Dario, Lodovico,
Matteo, Riccardo and all those who love Siena

Introduction

A Guide to Siena for the very young

The spirit of a community continues to live if it passes on its historical events, its cultural heritage, and its memories in appropriate ways.

It is not a cliché to say that amongst the many cities in our country, Siena is certainly one of the richest in these elements. It has, moreover, a collective fabric of local realities, the Contradas whose roots make them the most motivated, passionate and untiring caretakers.

In this network of relationships, special attention is paid to the young, who not only in school, but also in the multileveled local society must find reasons to be included in the local reality in a positive way. We consider this inclusion successful if it is done with knowledge and with awareness, that is, the recognizing environment where they live as their own, and finding every means to protect its truest values.

But it is not simple to find the tools for this job of raising the young. Todays society much more often looks at them as targets for constantly increasing needs and consumption, rather than as generous organisms open to improving themselves intellectually and socially. When these tools are offered to a public of young people, not to mention to the very young, it is truly the entire society which takes a step forward.

Siena is a splendid city, endowed with innumerable cultural, artistic and environmental riches. And so it appears to the very numerous, admiring visitors from all coutries of the world who visit it nowadays in all periods of the year. Each one of them leafs through a guidebook of its attractions, in many different languages, with different illustrations and suggested visits.
Those who do not have a guidebook, be it concise, be it brief, -or those who are not culturally prepared - are excluded almost automatically from an understanding of the city.

But the generations of young people who see these interested crowds pass through their city, will have asked themselves what attracts them, what the buildings mean, these images that they always have in front of them. Perhaps they cannot imagine what makes these familiar things so attractive and important.

Here, finally is a guidebook of Siena for children, one with simple but thorough texts, as this task requires. This is not as easy as it seems, because to adapt its language to that of the youngest reader, requires a well-controlled effort of attention and a discipline in the use of terminology on the part of Mèsy Bartoli and Barbara Latini and the effective illustrations of Monica Verdiani.

This book, published by Betti Publishing Co., works to fill a long-standing gap, and addresses a public that is *tabula rasa*, and who, exactly for this reason, will enjoy with the enthusiasm of young organisms the text which brings them closer to the events of their own city, to its most relevant aspects, and to its most living traditions, without neglecting to explain the terminology - at times difficult - of their artistic heritage and illustrating the iconography of sacred characters who so often present in works of art.

Next to family and scholastic training, this permanent educational tool for the very young seems to me of great interest and indispensable for arousing, even in the youngest generations, a more profound connection and a more motivated affection for their city.

Bruno Santi
Superintendent for Artistic and Historic Works of Siena

Table of Contents

Legend

 Look in the dictionary

(☞ p. xxx) Go to page

 Write the answer

Hi! Let me introduce myself. I'm the **BALzana**, the coat of arms of the city of Siena, but you can call me **BAL** for short. I was born many, many years ago from a beautiful legend that I'm going to tell you and I have lived in this city forever. The Sienese love me and spoil me and when they have something important to celebrate they always save a place for me in the front row.

If you raise your head up really high as you walk around the streets of Siena, you'll see me poking out of the windows of the most beautiful palaces or on the columns of some famous monuments. Often I even wave from the top of the Torre del Mangia. Naturally, over the years from these positions I've learned a lot of secrets and curious things about my city.

Do you want to know some of them? Just follow me. I have lots of surprising things to show you.

8

Here's what you will find in this guidebook:

 A **SMALL MAP** of Siena with drawings of the most important monuments

The **HISTORY** of Siena so we can take a trip in time together

 Three **ROUTES** to visit the city

The **PALIO** and the **CONTRADAS**

  Some strange stories about the lives of the **ARTISTS** and the **SAINTS**

A **SMALL DICTIONARY** that explains the most difficult words, the ones that are followed in the text with a little star

Pay attention! Every time you see me I will have something very important to say to you!

If you've got your most comfortable shoes on and are carrying a camera, you're ready to begin.
Let's get going.....

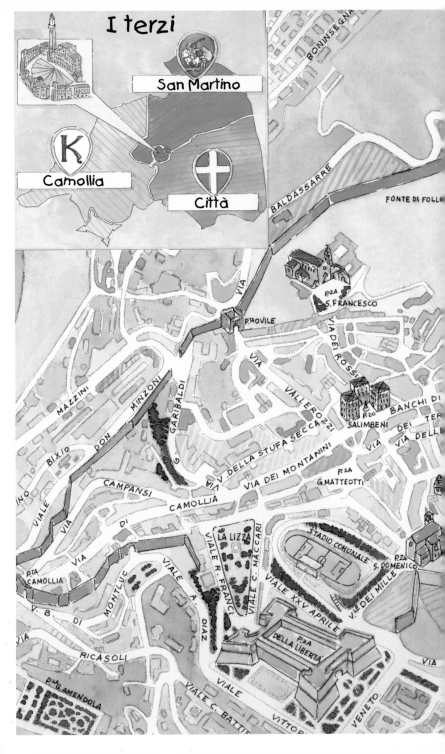

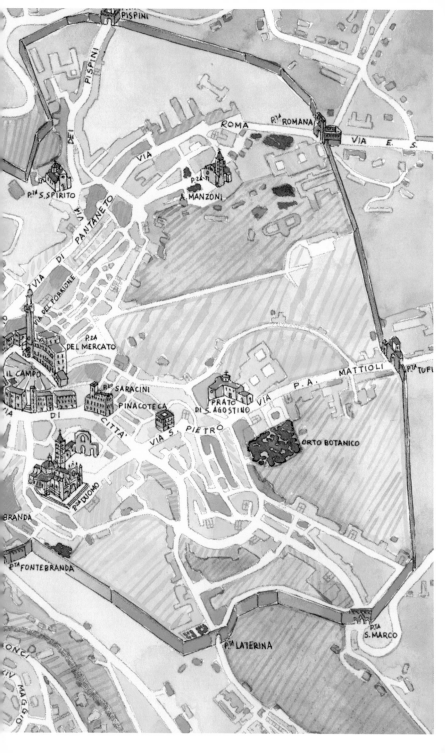

Remember that when we talk about a century we refer to the previous 100 years, for example, the 13th century is a period going from 1201 to the year 1300. Instead, when I speak about the 1300s, I mean 1301-1399.

Etruscan Village

Siena becomes a Roman military colony called "Saena Julia"

Jesus is born

Martyrdom of St Ansanus

Lombard domination;
Development of the Via Francigena

Rule by the Franks

Foundation of the Hospital of Santa Maria della Scala

Siena is a rich and powerful Free City

Government of the Twenty-four

Battle of Montaperti: Siena defeats Florence

Battle of Colle Val d'Elsa: Florence "beats" Siena

Government of the Nine.
Period of greatest splendor of the City;
the building of the Palazzo Pubblico (Town Hall)

St Catherine of Siena is born

The Plague; more than half of the population dies

Giangaleazzo Visconti, the Duke of Milan, governs the city

Saint Bernardine preaches for the first time in Piazza del Campo

Enea Silvio Piccolomini becomes Pope Pius II

Foundation of Monte di Pietà (Monte dei Paschi)

Siena is a Signoria governed by the "Magnificent" Pandolfo Petrucci

Battle of Porta Camollia: Siena defeats the army of the Pope, who is allied with the Florentines

War of Siena: the city, allies of the French, loses to the Spanish, allies of the Florentines

Cosimo dei Medici obtains feudal possession of Siena

Fall of the Sienese Republic in retreat in Montalcino; the Sienese State passes definitively to the Medici

The first Palio race is run in the Piazza del Campo

Violante of Bavaria establishes the number of the Contradas (17) and their boundaries

End of the Medici dynasty; the Grand Duchy of Tuscany passes to the Hapsburg Lorena

Inauguration of the railroad (Siena - Empoli line)

Siena is the first Tuscan city to vote for the Unification of Italy

Destruction and Reconstruction of the Salicotto quarter

Foundation of the Accademia Musicale Chigiana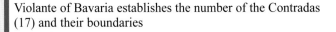

Second World War: Siena is declared a "hospital city" and is not bombed

Cultural, scientific, and tourist development

St Catherine of Siena is named Patron Saint of Europe

History

The origins of Siena

Many legends exist about the origin of Siena. The most famous one says that in the 8th Cent. B.C. **SENIUS** and **ASCHIUS**, sons of Remus, ran away from Rome and from their cruel Uncle Romulus. When they left they took away with them the famous statue of the She-wolf that had nursed the twins.

They ran far, far away and and finally stopped when they reached the Tressa river. There some shepherds helped them build a castle they called Castelvecchio and slowly a city began to grow up around it. Because Aschius and Senius wanted to thank the gods Apollo and Diana for protecting them during their escape, they lit large fires on two altars. The smoke was white over the altar of Apollo, but black over the altar of Diana. And so, they decided that these would be the colors of the coat of arms of the city they founded. And that's how Siena and I - **Bal** - were born!

But let's leave the legend behind and have a look at the history.
Then we'll begin our journey.

In the time of the **ETRUSCANS** (6th Cent. B.C.) Siena was an important village located in the area where now you find the Spedale di Santa

Maria della Scala. Later it became part of the great **ROMAN EMPIRE** and during the rule of Octavius Augustus (29 B.C.) it was a **MILITARY COLONY** called *Saena Iulia*. Siena grew and became a city with palaces, markets, and thermal baths. Even today the names of some streets help us understand what the city might have been like in the

time of the Romans. For example, in via delle Terme (Street of the Thermal Baths) there must have been buildings for bathing, and in via del Porrione, a name which comes from the Latin word *emporium*, there must have been a market! However Siena was always a long way away from the main Roman roads, like the via Cassia and the via Aurelia and this kept it from becoming a great city of the Empire.

Also for this reason, **CHRISTIANITY** didn't spread throughout the city until the 4th Cent. A.D., when **ST ANSANUS**. (p. 113) arrived in Siena.

Did you know… that you can find interesting Etruscan and Roman remains in the NATIONAL ARCHAEOLOGICAL MUSEUM of Siena? (See if you can find them; the Museum's inside the Hospital of Santa Maria della Scala.)

Siena in the Middle Ages

After the fall of the Roman Empire, Italy was invaded by barbaric populations. The **Lombards** settled in Tuscany and during their domination (7th-8th Cent. A.D.) Siena became smaller compared to what it was in the Roman period. The houses were concentrated near the hills of Castelvecchio and Santa Maria (where the Cathedral stands today). In Castelvecchio you still see some streets with names of Lombard origins. Via Stalloreggi, for example, comes from *stabulum regi*, which means "stalla del Re" (stable of the

King). Under the Lombards (and then also under the **Franks**) Italy was crossed from the north down to Rome by an important road that was called the *Francigena* because it came down from France.

Knights, merchants, pilgrims, and robbers all traveled the **via Francigena** (☞ p. 71). This road passed through Siena, coming in through Porta Camollia and going out through Porta Romana. And it influenced Siena's growth as a city. After the year 1000 Siena expanded from its original area around Castelvecchio and built a series of castellari along the via Francigena. These fortified structures later formed the **Terzi**, or Thirds, into which the city is still divided today: *the Terzo di Camollia, the Terzo di San Martino, and the Terzo di Città*. This is why Siena is called the 'daughter of the road'... have a look at the small map for a moment and you'll understand.

Whoever traveled the via Francigena and passed through Siena could find hospitality and medical care in many places of shelter. The largest of these was the SPEDALE 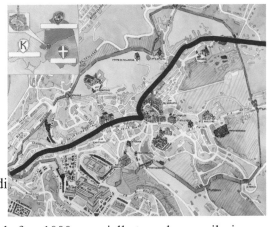 di SANTA MARIA DELLA SCALA, which was built before 1000 especially to welcome pilgrims (☞ p. 72) and travelers.

In the 12th century Siena became a FREE CITY like other Italian cities and was governed by the CAPTAIN OF THE PEOPLE, by the CONSULS and by the PODESTÀ (Magistrate). However in Siena there were also the COUNCIL OF THE BELL, the citizen parliament that gathered together at the sound of a bell, and the BALÌA, a group of important people who came together only in times of emergency. In addition, two offices administered the money: the BICCHERNA Office took care of the expenses of the city, and the GABELLA (Tax) OFFICE collected the taxes. In the 1200s Siena was rich and powerful thanks to commerce and to its ability to lend money to popes and kings. It also already had its own UNIVERSITY.

During this period when everything seemed to go well, the city began to expand its boundaries by fighting against nearby cities, especially Florence. And the powerful Sienese families even fought for power

17

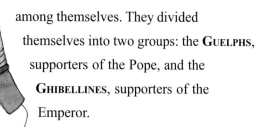 among themselves. They divided themselves into two groups: the **GUELPHS**, supporters of the Pope, and the **GHIBELLINES**, supporters of the Emperor.

In 1260, under the **GOVERNMENT OF THE TWENTY-FOUR** (Ghibelline), the **BATTLE OF MONTAPERTI** was fought against the Florentines. On the night before the battle, the Sienese asked the Madonna for protection and offered her the keys to the city. That is how that the Virgin Mary became the "queen" of Siena. The victory of the Sienese army was overwhelming, and it guaranteed the city supremacy over Tuscany. But the glory didn't last long. In 1269, in fact, with the **BATTLE OF COLLE VAL D'ELSA**, the Sienese were defeated by the Florentines.
sconfitti dai Fiorentini.

Later the **GOVERNMENT OF THE NINE** (Guelph) was formed, "nine" being the number of merchants and bankers who governed the city for about 70 years, from 1287 to 1355.

This long period of time was one of the happiest times for the Republic of Siena. The PALAZZO PUBBLICO (Town Hall) was built with its TORRE DEL MANGIA (Mangia Tower)and the NEW DUOMO (Cathedral) was planned. The whole city was enriched with works of art

Unfortunately, in 1348 a terrible plague, called the **BLACK DEATH**, spread throughout all of Europe. Siena also suffered. In fact, more than half of the population died. For the Republic this was the beginning of a slow economic and political decline. The Sienese entrusted the government of the city to an outsider, **GIAN GALEAZZO VISCONTI,** the Duke of Milan, however he was not able to bring back to Siena the splendor of the past!

The End of the Republic

In the middle of the 1400s the Sienese Enea Silvio Piccolomini was elected Pope with the name of **Pius II** and once again Siena enjoyed cultural richness. The city was beautified with important monuments, like the Logge del Papa. Pienza, the ideal city of the Renaissance, also owes its extraordinary beauty and its name to Pius II!

In 1472 Monte di Pietà, an institution for lending money, was born. In the 1600s it became the **Monte dei Paschi** bank. The origin of the word 'paschi' refers to the fact that in the beginning of its activity, this banking institution got its money from the rental of

'pascoli' (pastures) in Maremma.

At the end of the same century, Siena became a **Signoria** and Pandolfo Petrucci the Magnificent, took control of the city. The Sienese did not like this government and after 'the Magnificent' died, the Petrucci family was no longer able to command the city. During the early years of the 1500s, when the largest European countries tried to expand their borders toward Italy, Siena was a city that other people fought over. Pope Clement VII, with the support of the Florentines, tried to get control of the city, but his army was defeated by the Sienese in the **BATTLE OF PORTA CAMOLLIA**. Some years later Emperor Charles V, again with the support of the Florentines, tried to conquer Siena. The imperial army besieged the city, the beginning move of the historic **WAR OF SIENA**.

The battle was hard-fought, and to resist the enemy the Sienese decided to send the women, the old people, the sick and the children (the 'useless mouths') far away from the city. However, all their efforts were for nothing. In 1555 Siena was defeated and Emperor Charles V named the powerful Florentine **COSIMO I DEI MEDICI** the Grand Duke of Tuscany and Master of Siena. But it wasn't until 1559 that the glorious Republic of Siena, which had retreated to Montalcino, actually fell. The Medici had a great **FORTEZZA** (fortress) built at the gates of the city. On the ramparts of the fortress and on the façades of the most important buildings the Florentines placed the Medici coat of arms as a symbol of the power of this family in the city. The coat of arms is in the form of a shield with six balls. These 'balls' might represent pills, since the founder of the family was, in fact, a doctor.

Siena from the Grand Duchy to the Unification of Italy

The Medici family ruled all of Tuscany until the 18th century. Under the government of Giangastone, the last heir of the Medici family, the Governor of Siena, Violante of Bavaria, approved the REGULATIONS that defined the BOUNDARIES of the CONTRADAS and fixed their NUMBER at 17. This 'regulation' is still valid today. Giangastone died without heirs and the throne of Tuscany passed to the family of the HAPSBURG LORENA.

In the 1800s Siena began to adjust to the scientific developments

of the century and built, for example, the first line of the RAILROAD or 'iron road' that arrived in Empoli.

In 1860 Siena was also the first Tuscan city to vote to be united with the Kingdom of Italy.

The 1900s

In the beginning of the 1900s Siena was still a small provincial city. During this time poverty, disease, and unemployment were serious problems in the city. Many families had to live in old houses, where the sanitary conditions were terrible.

During the years of **FASCISM**  entire quarters, like the Salicotto neighborhood, were completely knocked down and rebuilt. New quarters for the people were built outside the walls on the hill of Ravacciano and in the Valli area. Two institutions were founded: the **UNIVERSITÀ PER STRANIERI**, and the **ACCADEMIA MUSICALE CHIGIANA**, which today is famous throughout the world. During the **SECOND WORLD WAR**, Siena was declared a HOSPITAL CITY and, for the most part, was spared from the bombings. Thanks to a 'special law' (1963) that protects the monuments of Siena, the city has kept the MEDIEVAL LOOK you can still admire today!

Important and ancient institutions, like the **UNIVERSITY**, the **GENERAL HOSPITAL**, and the **MONTE DEI PASCHI BANK** of Siena have brought improvements and well-being to the city. And it has become a very important TOURIST DESTINATION. Every year millions of tourists come to visit.

That brings us up to the present and the end of our long journey through time.

So let's begin our visit to the city, starting from **Piazza del Campo**.

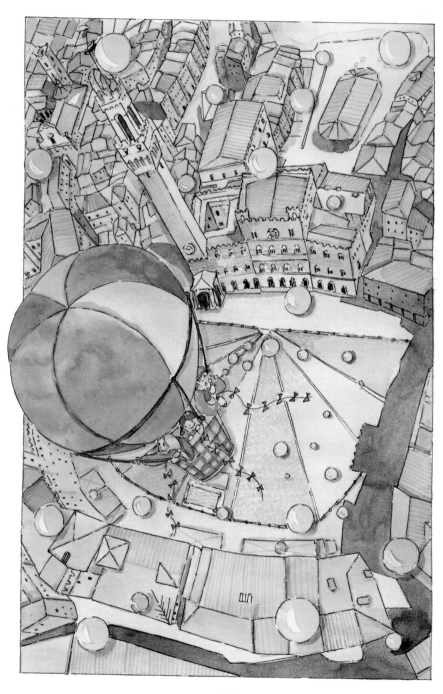

24

Have you ever been aboard a hot air balloon? Climb on board with me and we'll fly over the city! Hold on tight. Lift offffffff.......

What you see down below is the PIAZZA DEL CAMPO, one of the most beautiful squares in the world. It's located in the center of the Thirds and is the heart of Siena and of the Sienese.

A long long time ago the Piazza was not a big scallop shell like it is today. Try to imagine instead a meadow large enough to hold markets and fairs, assemblies and festivals. The Palazzo Pubblico (Town Hall) and the other buildings were not yet built. In the 12th Century an enormous wall was set up which separated Piazza del Campo from what today is the Piazza del Mercato. Around this wall were the Customs building and the Bolgano - the Mint of Siena - where money was coined ⭐. These buildings later became part of the Town Hall.

Don't forget that the via Francigena (☞ p. 71) ran along the edge of the CAMPO. So naturally there was a lot of commercial activity in the Piazza. During the rule of the GOVERNMENT OF THE NINE the Sienese made the Piazza more beautiful. They paved it with bricks and divided it into nine sections with eight stripes of white marble. Can you count them? They probably did this in honor of the Nine who governed the city.

1 - Palazzo Pubblico (town hall)
2 - San Martino
3 - Palazzo Chigi Zondadari
4 - Palazzo Sansedoni
5 - Sede della Mercanzia (Casin dei Nobili)
(Merchants' Headquarters)
6 - Costarella dei Barbieri
7 - Palazzo Alessi - d'Elci
8 - Casato
9 - Fonte Gaia (Fountain of Joy)

Today the outside part of the Piazza is made of stone and during the Palio horse race it is covered with tufa sand ⭐.

In the 1300s a FOUNTAIN was built (☞ p.90). It was called **GAIA** (Joyful) because the arrival of water in the Piazza del Campo made the Sienese so happy and joyful. In 1419 they replaced it with an larger and more beautiful one sculpted by Jacopo della Quercia (☞

p.110). Over time, water, wind and smog ruined this masterpiece and the one you see today is a work done in the 1800s by the sculptor Tito Sarrocchi (☞ p. 111). You can still see some of the wonderful original

marble statues by Jacopo della Quercia today inside the SPEDALE DI SANTA MARIA DELLA SCALA. Later on we'll go have a look!!!

Did you know that.... the Palio horse race is run twice a year in this Piazza? (☞ p. 92)

The big palace that we are flying over now is **PALAZZO PUBBLICO**, the most important one in the city. It was built between the end of the 1200s and the beginning of the 1300s to house the **NINE** who governed the Republic of Siena. Other public offices, like the the Customs office and the Bolgano (the Mint), had already existed in this place for a long time and these were later added to the construction of the new building.

Originally the Palazzo was very small. It included only the four central stone arches in the form of what are called Sienese arches  because they were invented right in this city. Later, other parts were added: the side sections, the upper floors in red brick and the crown with nine Guelph merlons , one for each governor of the Republic. Palazzo Pubblico, built in the Gothic style (☞ p. 100), is decorated with many large windows called trifores .

Look in the center of the arch. See anything familiar? It's me - the **BALZANA**!

The small bell tower high up on your right held the 'martinella'. This was the bell they used to ring in times of danger to warn the armies of the TERZI to get ready for battle. The small bell tower on your left was added in the 1600s and so were the upper floors of the two side sections. On the façade, just under the merlons, there is a large sun that encircles three letters, **'JHS'**, which means 'Jesus, Saviour of Men' This symbol was used by Saint Bernardine of Siena (☞ p. 113) who showed it to the crowd during his sermons. It became the custom at that time to put it over the doors of houses, churches and public buildings to obtain the protection of Jesus.

Now, look down at the big stone shield. That's the coat of arms of the Medici family which ruled Siena for a long time. Still today this building is the **PALAZZO DEL COMUNE** (Town Hall).

La Torre del Mangia

The tall elegant **TORRE** to the side of the Palazzo Pubblico is called **DEL**

MANGIA, from the nickname of the bell-ringer. Giovanni di Balduccio, better known as MANGIAGUADAGNI (money-eater) or MANGIA, was appointed by the Town to strike the hours. At the top of the tower there is a large bell that the Sienese call CAMPANONE O SUNTO (Big Bell of the Assumption) because it is dedicated to the Assumption of the Virgin. The tower was built between 1338 and 1348.

Do you know how tall it is?

87 meters or 102 meters if you count the lightning rod. You can climb to the top, but you have to have an adult with you!

Chapel on the square

The **CHAPEL** at the foot of the Torre del Mangia was built by the Sienese in the middle of the 14th century to thank the Madonna for bringing an end to the plague of 1348. It is made of white marble and decorated all over with niches , statues and garlands

Now, let's land and visit the inside of the Palazzo

We enter through the **COURTYARD OF THE PODESTÀ**. On your left is the entrance to the Torre del Mangia and on the opposite side is the entrance to the **CIVIC MUSEUM**. Inside this museum I'll show you some of the most important masterpieces of Sienese art.

Remember that it is FORBIDDEN to take photographs inside the museum!!!

Let's begin the visit in the big hall whose ceiling and walls are all decorated. All around you there are scenes of soldiers, battles and great ceremonies.

This is the SALA DEL RISORGIMENTO , which was completed at the end of the 1800s to celebrate the first king of United Italy, Victor Emmanuel II. Do you know who the two people on horseback shaking hands are? The one on the black horse is Garibaldi; the other one on the white horse is King Victor Emmanuel II. As you leave the hall, you'll see a staircase on your left that leads to the upper floors. Let's go! Up here is the large LOGGIA where the NINE would walk about. The view from the loggia is very beautiful, isn't it?

Go back down the stairs and head for the SALA DI BALÌA (Hall of Power). Look at the BIG CHAIRS where the Balìa sat. Remember them? They were that group of rules who met only in times of emergency. The frescos (☞ p. 40) on the walls tell the *History of Pope Alexander III*, who helped the City defeat Emperor Frederick Barbarossa. Spinello Aretino (☞ p. 111) painted them in the early 1400s

Can you spot....

Look closely at this picture of battle. Which wall can you find it on? (☞ 1 p. 122)

32

After you go through a few other rooms, you'll come to the big SALA DEL MAPPAMONDO (Hall of the Map of the World). It got its name from a large revolving map of the territory of Siena. Now this map is lost, but until the 18th Cent. it was found on the wall to your right. If you look carefully, you can see the marks that the rotating map left on the wall! The fresco above it is called *Guidoriccio da Fogliano during the Siege of the Castle of Montemassi* and it was done by the Sienese painter Simone Martini (☞ p. 105) in 1328. The elegant knight was the captain of the Sienese army. Look at that! The knight and his horse have on the same *uniform*!!! On your left the painter showed the rebel castle of Montemassi, which Guidoriccio conquered for the Sienese Republic. In the center there is a small wooden fort with a catapult. Imagine what kind of big boulders that could launch! The group of tents on the right represents the camp of the Sienese army.

How can you recognize that the tents belong to soldiers from Siena? (☞ 2 p. 122)

Did you know that....

the castle that you see under Guidoriccio was hidden for centuries by a layer of plaster? It was discovered during some restoration work and is so beautiful that scholars consider it a work of the great Sienese painter Duccio di Buoninsegna (☞ p. 104).

33

On the wall to your left there is a wonderful *Maestà* ⭐, another fresco by Simone Martini which he did a few years before *Guidoriccio*. The Madonna, with the Christ child in her arms, sits under a canopy that is supported by eight saints and decorated with the Balzana. All around them there are angels and saints. In the foreground two angels offer the Madonna baskets full of flowers. Kneeling on the sides of the Virgin are the four patron saints of Siena. From the left, you can see St Ansanus, St Sabinus, St Crescentius and St Victor (☞ p. 113-115). Simone Martini painted in a very elegant and refined way. Look at how sweet the faces of the people are and how richly decorated their clothes are! Can you see what makes the painting sparkle? The painter used gold leaf in the halo and in the throne of the Madonna to show that this was the kingdom of heaven.

What doesn't belong?

Look carefully at the picture of the *Maestà* and you will discover something quite out of place! (☞ 3 p. 122)

Now I going to point out something a bit strange. Raise your eyes toward the ceiling. There are two *hands* painted on wood that are used to hold the chains of the votive lamps ⭐. Can you see them?

Now let's go into the **Sala della Pace** (Hall of Peace), where the Nine received their most important guests. The frescos that decorate the walls represent the merits of GOOD GOVERNMENT by which the Nine tried to govern the city. The Nine commissioned  the frescos from the Sienese artist Ambrogio Lorenzetti (☞ p. 109) who painted them between 1337 and 1339. Look for a moment at *The Allegory*  *of Good Government* on the right wall. The picture is dominated by the big figure of an elderly man dressed in a black and white tunic.

What do you think this represents? (☞ 4 p. 122)

At his feet there is a She-wolf with twins and sitting at the side of the old lord as counsellors, there are some strange women. The first is *Peace* in a white dress; she wears a crown of laurel and holds an olive branch. Next comes *Fortitude*, who holds a scepter and a shield. *Prudence* is pictured with a mirror. *Magnanimity*  holds a crown in her hand and a plate full of money on her lap. *Temperance*  has an hourglass in her hands. Finally, there is *Justice*, who is pictured with a sword and the decapitated head of a criminal. To the left there is another image of *Justice*, which is absolutely necessary in a well-governed city.

Now turn around to the right. You are standing in front of the *Effects of Good Government in the City and the Countryside.*

This is Siena in the 1300s. Did you imagine it like this?

The painter showed the city with its towers, palaces, bell towers and the dome of the Cathedral. Are you able to see them? Under a "Good Government", it's nice to live in the city.

Have a look at the people. Some bricklayers are building a palace, a shoemaker is working in his workshop, a teacher is teaching his students and a weaver is working at his loom. There's even a wedding

parade with the bride on horseback and her ladies-in-waiting dancing together behind her.

In the center of the scene a large gate opens towards the countryside. This is Porta Romana. Look carefully at this Tuscan landscape. You can see some farmers harvesting grain and others working in the

vineyards. There are also hunters and woodsmen. With a "Good Government" it is also nice to live in the countryside!

Now have a look at the opposite wall. This is the *Allegory of Bad Government and its Effects on the City and the Countryside.*

The scene is dominated by a horrible character with the horns of a bull and the fangs of a wild boar. This is *Tyranny*, who holds a dagger and a cup of poison. Other terrible characters sit at his side as counsellors:

Cruelty shows a serpent to the baby she's holding; *Deception* holds an animal with the head of a lamb and the tail of a snake; *Fraud* has the wings of a bat and holds a club;

Fury is a centaur with the head of a wild pig and the tail of a wolf; *Discord*, dressed in white and black, tries to saw herself in two; *War* holds a shield and a sword. And lying on the ground below them is poor *Justice* with a broken pair of scales.

On your left are the effects of this bad government. The fresco is quite ruined, but you can see soldiers, dead people, and buildings which have collapsed. The streets are covered with rubbish, the shops are deserted and the fields are burned. The colors are dull and the atmosphere is very sad, don't you think?

Who are these characters? (☞ 5 p. 122)

And now, go into the **Sala del Concistoro** (Hall of the Assembly) where you can have a look at the ceiling with frescos by Domenico Beccafumi (☞ p. 111)

We've come to the end of our visit to the Civic Museum. But before leaving the Palazzo Pubblico, I suggest you visit the Salt Warehouse. Don't be afraid; there aren't any ghosts or goblins. Only big rooms where the City of Siena kept their store of supplies during the Middle Ages. Did you know that salt especially was very precious at that time?

Would you like to color
the knight Guidoriccio da Fogliano?

How to make...a fresco

A FRESCO is one of the most important techniques of painting. It had a great development in the Italian art of the 1300s and during all of the Renaissance period (☞ p. 102). In the 1300s this type of painting was done by spreading a layer of plaster called ARRICCIO (2) on the WALL (1). A painter then traced his design with a red ochre color called SINOPIA ⭐ (3). Over this drawing he spread another thin transparent layer called PLASTER FINISH (4). Finally, the painter

applied the color (5). When it came in contact with the fresh lime and the air, the color became dry and inseparable from the wall. At that point it was no longer possible to erase mistakes!

In the Renaissance a painter did a life-size drawing on a piece of cardboard, and then punched the cardboard with holes along the outline of the figure. When he placed this cartoon against the wall and passed carbon powder over the holes, it left an outline on the wall.

The part of the fresco done in one days time was called a "giornata" or a "day's work".

How to make.... Colors

In the Middle Ages and in the Renaissance painters made their own colors with what nature offered. Often the colors had strange names and were a sort of concoction of stones, leaves, and ground berries mixed with water and egg white - almost as if the painters were bakers. Each painter and every workshop had their own "recipe" to obtain colors that were brilliant and resistant over time.

Here are some ingredients used to obtain the most frequently used colors.

BLACK: To get black you burned branches of grapevines or peach-stones or else you used charcoal.

RED: To get a red called *dragon's blood* you used the resin of a palm tree.

YELLOW: To obtain a *yellow ochre* clay was used; *giallorino* required lead and a yellow color called *risalgallo* was produced with the poison arsenic.

GREEN: To get a beautiful *bright green* the mineral malachite was ground and for a *darker green* verdigris was used. Other shades of green were obtained by mixing yellow with blue.

WHITE: For white they used lime "shaked" in water and got *St John white*. Another type of white was obtained by grinding animal bone and it was called *bone-white*.

BLUE: One kind of blue was called *della Magna* because it arrived from the country of Alemagna, which we now call Germany. They got ultramarine *blue* by grinding lapis lazuli stones. For this reason it was very precious and expensive.

This route will help you discover the oldest district of the city: Castelvecchio

We start out from the Church of San Pietro alle Scale and head towards the hill of Castelvecchio. After a steep climb we arrive at a CASTELLARE. This is the best preserved of all the existing ones in Siena. Go through the entrance with the two arches overhead and you'll find yourself in a courtyard. Originally the castellare was a wooden or stone enclosure that included one

or more towers. Inside, as you can still see today, there was a courtyard surrounded by houses, warehouses, stables and sometimes even a church. Rich families built this type of fortress and lived there with their servants. Go on now along the *vicolo di Castelvecchio* and at the end of the street you'll come to the

CHURCH OF THE CARCERI DI SANT' ANSANO (Prison of St Ansanus).

According to legend, St Ansanus (☞ p.113), the first martyr of the city, was imprisoned here. Ansanus baptized the Sienese who converted to Christianity from the small window in the tower.

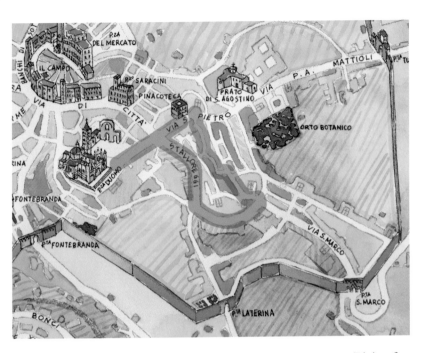

Go down towards the left until you reach **Pian dei Mantellini** (Plain of Little Mantles). The name came from the very short mantles worn by the monks of the old convent of the church in front of you, the Church of San Niccolò al Carmine. When you arrive at **Due Porte** (Two Gates), walk through the arch and you will be in *via Stalloreggi*. On your right you'll find the building where the **workshop** (☞ p. 60) of **Duccio di Buoninsegna** (☞ p. 104) used to be. Right here the famous Sienese painter painted the *Maestà* ⭐ and on 9 June 1311 the people of Siena carried it all the way to the Cathedral in a grand procession.

45

A little bit ahead is the **Tabernacle** ⭐ **of the Madonna of the Crow.** Legend says that it was built in 1348 on the spot where a dead crow fell to the ground and spread a terrible plague throughout the city. Along this street, like in other areas of the city, there are many TOWER HOUSES. This type of tall narrow house didn't offer a comfortable life, but it did guarantee protection and prestige for the people who lived there.

The "tower house" was a stone building whose door was very narrow and higher than the street. People entered using a wooden stairway that could be removed in times of danger. The windows were small and let in very little light.

On the façade of the "tower house", like on those of other medieval buildings, you can see small SQUARE HOLES. They aren't pigeon houses, but the PONTAIE HOLES where wooden poles were inserted to support scaffolding or a projecting type of balcony. The "balconies" were used to move from one tower to another without having to go down to ground level, but they were also very useful for shooting arrows and pouring boiling oil down on the enemy.

When you arrive at PIAZZA DI POSTIERLA, or **QUATTRO CANTONI** (Four Corners) as the Sienese call it, turn right and you will come to Palazzo Buonsignori. This palace is the home of the **PINACOTECA** ⭐ (National Picture Gallery) (see the photograph), one of the most important Italian museums. If you like painting, go in and look around a bit. You"ll find the unique precious paintings with their "gold background" (☞ p. 63) that have made Sienese and Italian painting famous. There are masterpieces by Duccio di Buoninsegna, Simone Martini, Pietro and Ambrogio Lorenzetti, Francesco di Giorgio Martini, Domenico Beccafumi, and Rutilio Manetti (☞ p. 111), to name only the most famous.

Let's go back to Quattro Cantoni and continue our walk along VIA DEL CAPITANO. On this street is the beautiful **PALAZZO DEL CAPITANO**, built in stone and brick, with Sienese arches  and biforate windows typical of the Gothic style (☞ p. 100). Once it was the residence of the Captain of War and Justice. Let's go on:

Here we are in Piazza del Duomo.

The **Duomo** or CATHEDRAL is dedicated to the Madonna and was built in the 12th century where there once had been a much more ancient church. According to tradition, it was consecrated in 1179 by Pope Alexander III. However, even this second building soon turned out to be too small for the ever-growing population. Already in the 1200s they began work on a new building that was to be paid for by the City and by the Opera di Santa Maria (cathedral works council). The Gothic Cathedral that you see now is the result of the work of great artists like Nicola and Giovanni Pisano (☞ p. 106-107). Remember that in the 1300s Siena had become a very important city. To demonstrate its power it wanted to build a NEW CATHEDRAL

48

which would be the most beautiful in Italy, but more importantly, bigger than the one in Florence!

According to the plan, the building that we see today would have been the short arm, or the transept , of the new Cathedral. Imagine the size! Work was begun, but things didn't exactly go as expected. In 1348 the plague reduced the population by half. This put the city, which was financing the project, in serious economic difficulty. The work was suspended. The FACCIATONE (Large façade), the tall construction that stands along one side of PIAZZA JACOPO DELLA QUERCIA, is all that remains today of that ambitious building.

The City abandoned their plan for the New Cathedral, but decided to go on with work on the old Cathedral. Even this took quite a while.

Let's have a closer look at the façade:

It is made of white and dark green marble, with three PORTALS , GABLES and SPIRES typical of the Gothic style. It was planned by Giovanni Pisano (☞ p. 107), one of the most important sculptors of that time. The same artist also sculpted the many statues of prophets and sibyls that decorate the façade. In the 1800s these statues were substituted by copies; you can find the originals in the Museo dell' Opera. The sides of the Cathedral and the bell tower are decorated in stripes of white and black marble in honor of the colors of the city. The large dome is one of the oldest in Italy.

The **inside** of the Cathedral is in the form of a cross and is divided into a nave and two side aisles. The white and black stripes on the outside are also inside on the tall.

Treasure hunt: Before you go into the Cathedral, look carefully at these pictures and then see if you can find them inside. Write the matching number in the white spaces on the small map (☞ 6 p. 122).

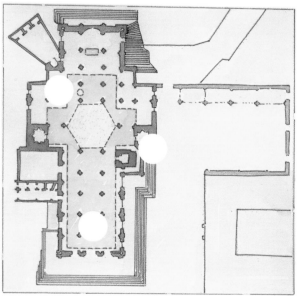

The inside of the Cathedral is in the form of a cross and is divided into a nave ⭐ and two aisles. The white and black stripes on the outside are also inside on the tall mighty columns that support the ceiling. And look, the ceiling even has little golden stars! The walls are rich with precious works of art.

Even the floor is a masterpiece. It is completely decorated with

precious INLAID marble (☞ p. 61). It looks like a carpet with prophets ⭐, sibyls ⭐, wise men and kings. Many scenes are covered so that they will not be ruined, but once a year they are uncovered for people to admire.

Notice how big the central nave is! If you walk towards the right transept , you'll come to the **CHAPEL OF OUR LADY OF THE VOW**, built in the full Baroque era (☞ p. 103). The residents of Siena are very devoted to the ancient painting above the altar in this chapel. It is a *Virgin with Child* from the Sienese School (☞ p. 101). In fact, do you see the many votive offerings hang on the wall outside the chapel? They are gifts that the faithful have left for the Virgin in appreciation for what they have received. Now walk under the large dome and turn towards the central nave.

Did you know that... you

can see two long wooden poles resting on two pillars? Tradition says they are the *pales* which belonged to the carroccio , the war cart used by the Sienese during the Battle of Montaperti.

Look now at the **high altar**. It was made in the 1500s by the architect Baldassarre Peruzzi (☞ p. 111) to take the place of the one which used to hold the *Maestà* of Duccio (☞ p. 104). The large round stained-glass window (☞ p. 62) above the apse ⭐ is the only one like it in the world. Duccio di Buoninsegna (☞ p. 104) designed it at the end of the 1200s. Its glass has remained intact for centuries and still today reflects a magical colored light.

On your left is the marble PULPIT ⭐ done in the 13th century by NICOLA PISANO with the help of his son Giovanni and of Arnolfo di Cambio (☞ p. 111). It is one of the masterpieces of Italian Gothic sculpture.

In the seven panels that make up the pulpit there are about 377 characters and about 70 animals. What a crowd! Don't you think they're a bit packed?

In the left transept you'll find the Renaissance style (☞ p. 102) CHAPEL OF ST JOHN THE BAPTIST, which was created to hold the relic ⭐ of the arm of the saint.

The large bronze statue is St John the Baptist by the Florentine sculptor Donatello (☞ p. 111).

The entrance to the **Piccolomini Library** is just ahead. The library was built to preserve the precious books belonging to Pope Pius II Piccolomini. The frescos on the walls were painted by the artist Pinturicchio (☞ p. 111) and show episodes from the life of the Sienese pope. Why don't you go in and look around a bit. The frescos (☞ p. 40) are so beautiful and colorful that they seem to have just come from the artist's paintbrush!

Before we end our visit, let's stop in front of the large white marble altar on your right.

This is the **Piccolomini altar** and the four statues on its sides were probably sculpted by Michelangelo (☞ p. 111), one of the greatest artists of all times.

Spedale di Santa Maria della Scala

Going out of the main doors of the Cathedral, you'll see a large building called the **Spedale di Santa Maria della Scala**, one of the oldest hospitals of the Middle Ages. The hospital was founded by the canons ⭐ of the Cathedral in the 11th century, even though a fanciful ancient legend says its foundation goes back to a shoemaker called Sorore. The name Santa Maria della Scala comes from

the fact that the façade of the Hospital is located precisely in front of the stairway (scala) of the Cathedral.

This Hospital was created to give shelter and help to travelers and pilgrims (☞ p. 72) who were going to Rome and to provide a place for the "gittatelli", or abandoned babies. Very soon, thanks to the money of the City and, above all, to the gifts of rich families, the Hospital became so large and important that it was almost "a city within a city". Santa Maria della Scala was so rich that it owned large fortified farms - *grance* - in the

countryside, which produced and preserved supplies of grain and other types of food.

During the 16th century the hospital was used less to help pilgrims and the poor and more to cure diseases and to take care of abandoned babies. Only in the 1800s did it become a hospital as we mean today. These days it is no longer a hospital. Instead, the City has been working since 1990 to transform this ancient building into a magnificent museum.

Go inside and you'll realize how big and beautiful it is. There are many, many things to discover. You'll enjoy yourself because it almost seems like you're in a labyrinth! Throughout your visit you'll find the coat of arms of the Spedale di Santa Maria della Scala represented many times.

See if you can find it and then
draw it!

Stop for a moment in the
Pilgrim's Hall. From the name
you probably understand that it
was right here that the pilgrims
who needed help were welcomed.
Look at the frescos ( p. 40)
that decorate the walls. On one
side are episodes from the *History
of the Hospital*. On the opposite
side are the *Works of Charity* towards the pilgrims, the abandoned
babies, and the sick.

These frescos were done in the 1400s by famous Sienese artists like il
Vecchietta and Domenico di Bartolo (☞ p. 111).

Now go downstairs to visit the **Oratorio di Santa Caterina della
Notte** (St Catherine's night oratory). This is where the Saint stayed to
sleep after she had been here all day comforting the sick. In the
ancient **barn** you can see some of the original marble statues from the
Fonte Gaia (Fountain of Joy) sculpted by Jacopo della Quercia (☞ p.
110).

The Hospital also possesses a very precious *Treasury* which includes
antique golden jewel-cases studded with pearls and precious stones.
They contain very important relics ⭐ that people used to venerate
very much.

The **National Archeological Museum** is also inside the Hospital. If
you like archeology, you really should visit it!!!

Before you leave, don't forget to have a look at the **Church of the
Santissima Annuziata** and notice the beautiful golden coffered
ceiling ⭐.

Museo dell'Opera del Duomo

After you leave the Hospital, go to the **MUSEO DELL'OPERA**. The Opera della Metropolitana (OPA- is read *opera*) is an institution that has

always had the job of protecting and preserving the works of art of the Cathedral. In fact, the masterpieces that you can admire today in this museum used to be in the Cathedral. Let's start to discover some of the precious masterpieces. This first room is the **STATUE**

GALLERY where we can get close-up to the original sculptures from the façade of the Cathedral. Look at the statues of the prophets and the sibyls; do you see how their heads stick out? That was a trick of the sculptor Giovanni Pisano (☞ p. 107) to make the heads of the statues be seen better. Remember, at one time they were placed very high up!

On the next floor up (**HALL OF DUCCIO**) let's spend a bit more time looking at the extraordinary *Maestà* ⭐ by Duccio di Buoninsegna (☞ p. 104). This large painting on wood (☞ p. 63) was done between 1308 and 1311 for the high altar in the Cathedral, which at that time was located under the dome.

The *Maestà* was painted on two sides and had a frame, a predella ⭐ and gables. In fact, it resembled the façade of the Cathedral very much. In the 1700s the front and back sides of the painting were separated. When they did that, they destroyed the frame and lost some of the small panels. The missing pieces are preserved today in various

museums of the world.

Stop to examine the front side of the painting. Mary holds Baby Jesus in her arms and is sitting on a very elegant throne made of inlaid marble (☞ p. 61). At the base of the throne Duccio wrote his prayer: "O HOLY MOTHER OF GOD, BESTOW PEACE UPON SIENA, BESTOW LIFE UPON DUCCIO WHO PAINTED YOU IN THIS WAY". In the foreground you can see the four patron saints of Siena kneeling next to Mary: St Ansanus, St Sabinus, St Crescentius and St Victor (☞ p. 113-115). They are surrounded by a multitude of angels and saints. Do you see how much gold there is? Don't forget that the painter wanted to represent Paradise, the kingdom of the angels and the saints.

Memory quiz: Where did you see a Madonna on a throne with the four kneeling patron saints? (☞ 7 p. 122)

a) ❒ Piazza del Campo

b) ❒ Spedale di Santa Maria della Scala

c) ❒ Palazzo Pubblico

On the opposite wall of the hall you can see the back part of the painting which shows episodes from the Passion of Christ.

Now go up another floor and into the hall where they keep the *Madonna of the Big Eyes*. It was painted in the 13th century by the Maestro di Tressa, an anonymous painter of the Sienese School (☞ p. 101).

This Madonna gets its very unusual name from the fact that a long time ago the painting was surrounded by many silver ex-votive offerings whose round shape made them look like "big eyes". This is certainly the oldest and most sacred picture in Siena. In fact, precisely in front of this painting, on the night before the battle of Montaperti (1260), the Sienese prayed to the Madonna for help to win the battle against the Florentines.

Do you remember who won? (☞ 8 p. 122)

After you finish visiting the hall, you can climb up to the FACCIATONE and admire the beautiful panorama:

Don't forget to take a few nice photographs!

Once we've left the Museo dell'Opera del Duomo, let's go visit the BAPTISTRY ⭐.
To get to it you have to go down a steep staircase. Be careful -

don't run. On the eighth step you can see the sign of a cross. Right here, says a legend, St Catherine ( p. 112) was pushed by the devil and fell. So, watch out!

The Battistero

The **BATTISTERO** (baptistry) was built in the second half of the 1300s and is dedicated to St John the Baptist. If the planned work on the New Cathedral had been finished, the façade of the Battistero would have been one of the side entrances. Inside the Battistero there is a beautiful **BAPTISMAL** FONT done by important sculptors like Jacopo della Quercia and Donatello (p. 110-111).
If you like, you can have a look!!

This is the end of our first journey. If you have time to see more, I'd like to point out other monuments and important buildings that you can visit in this area:

THE CHURCH OF SANT' AGOSTINO, home of the Consorteria delle Compagnie Laicali di Siena
PALAZZO CHIGI SARACINI, home of the Accademia Musicale Chigiana
THE BOTANICAL GARDEN
PALAZZO DELLE PAPESSE, home of the Center of Contemporary Art

What is....a painter's workshop?

A **WORKSHOP** is the place where painters in the Middle Ages and the Renaissance worked. Whoever wanted to learn to be a painter went to the *workshop* of a famous artist. There, together with other students, he learned all the secrets of painting. In a painter's workshop there was always a lot to do: one person prepared the paintbrushes and the wooden panel for painting; someone else mixed the colors; someone drew and still another person cut the frames. The *maestro* took care of organizing the workshop, buying the materials, receiving the orders and collecting the money. When there were many pictures to paint, the *maestro* had his best students help him, but he always did the most important parts of the painting, like the faces or the hands himself. Many great painters learned in the workshops of other great painters. Giotto, for example, was in the workshop of Cimabue.

How to make.... an inlay of marble and semiprecious stones

An **INLAY** is similar to a mosaic. A model is prepared on thick paper, and then various-colored stones are cut in the shape of the design and fitted in one next to the other - just like in a *jigsaw puzzle*.

Lime is used to form a seal between the stones and stucco is used to finish the work. In this way you get a flat, smooth surface.

To make tarsia they used stones and marble of different colors - like white marble from Carrara, red marble from Grosseto, or green marble from Prato. Instead, for black, they use granite.

How to make....

a stained-glass window

To make the large **STAINED-GLASS WINDOWS** that you see in the churches the *master glassmaker* traced the life-size design on cardboard and the cut it up into many pieces as if it were a puzzle.

With a diamond tip he cut the colored GLASS into the shape he wanted and then put the various pieces together with strips of LEAD. It was a very delicate job! To get the greatest number of shades, pieces of glass with different colors were laid one on top of another. Some parts of the window, for example the faces and the clothing, were even painted, like in a real painting.

How to make....

a panel painting

To make a painting on wood the artist had to take boards of well-seasoned POPLAR WOOD and connect them together to get the size he wanted. Then he spread animal protein GLUE on the wood many times. This glue was gotten by boiling pieces of goat- or sheepskins in water. Next, he stretched strips of linen cloth which had been soaked in glue on the the glued board and then applied both a layer of THICK PLASTER and THIN PLASTER. Once it dried, he could trace the design directly onto the

board, or else on thick paper and transfer it to the surface with charcoal dust. In the Middle Ages it was very fashionable to have a background of GOLD-LEAF prepared by the gold-beater . The gold was glued with BOLE, a dark red clay, mixed with water and egg-white. The gilding was polished with a special instrument called a burnisher . The most important golden parts, like the halos, were made even more beautiful using a punch . Finally, the painting was polished with a special varnish which they put only on the parts that had been painted and never on the gold.

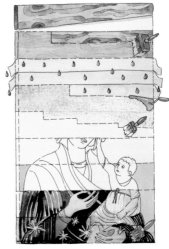

Let's begin our next journey inside the Terzo di San Martino.

We start out from the LOGGIA DELLA MERCANZIA (Porch of Commerce). This elegant Renaissance

architectural structure (☞ p. 102) was built in the first half of the 1400s. In the past the Juvenile Court held public hearings in this Loggia. Later, it became a meeting place of the rich lords of the city. But after the fall of the Republic (1555), the beautiful Loggia was a home for the stands of the treccoloni during the day and a shelter for homeless people during the night. In the niches above the large pillars you can see the statues of Saints Sabinus, Peter, Ansanus, Victor and Paul (☞ p. 113-115).

Take a guess:

Just a very quick game; can you guess this saint's name? (☞ 9 p. 122)

Now let's head toward the CROCE DEL TRAVAGLIO. In the Middle Ages this is the place where barricades of wooden beams were placed during popular rebellions. Nowadays

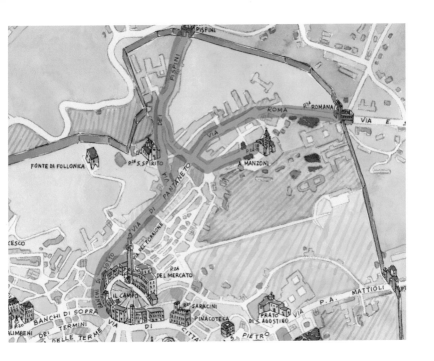

it is simply the meeting point of the "three" main streets of Siena: VIA DI CITTÀ, BANCHI DI SOPRA, and BANCHI DI SOTTO. Let's head first down **VIA BANCHI DI SOTTO**, an old part of the via Francigena (☞ p. 71).

A bit ahead on your right is the **PALAZZO PICCOLOMINI**. It's easy to recognize because it is a magnificent Renaissance building (☞ p. 102) with a stone façade and large windows with round arches ⭐. It was built in the second half of the 1400s for the Piccolomini family and today it is the home of the **STATE ARCHIVES**. Inside the Archives you can look things up in ancient documents and parchments or admire the precious Biccherna Covers (☞ p. 73), the painted wooden covers of the account books of the City of Siena.

Continuing down the street, the large portico you see on the right is the **Logge del Papa** (the Porch of the Pope). The Renaissance style (☞ p. 102) Logge, in white marble with large arches,

was built by the sculptor/architect Antonio Federighi (☞ p. 111) in the second half of the 15th century. The Logge was a gift from Pope Pius II Piccolomini to his family and the city of Siena.

Beside the Logge is the Church of San Martino. This was one of the first churches of Siena, but today nothing is left of its ancient structure.

The street that you see in front of you is VIA DEL PORRIONE. Do you remember what its name comes from? If you don't, just turn to page 15.

Before we continue our journey, I think we should wander around one of the many alleys that head down towards the **Salicotto quarter**. This area used to be the Jewish ghetto, which Cosimo I dei Medici created in the second half of the 1500s. The Jewish people remained in the ghetto ⭐ until the end of the 1700s.

Around 1930 almost all of the old houses of the district were demolished and replaced with more modern buildings. Even the Synagogue ⭐, which is found in this district, was restored at the beginning of the 1900s.

Did you know that... the name *Salicotto* comes from "sala-to" (salted) and "cotto" (cooked)? In the past a lot of salami was produced in this quarter.

Let's go on with our journey.

Shortly after the Logge del Papa, VIA BANCHI DI SOTTO becomes VIA PANTANETO. Perhaps this name comes from all the mud, also called "pantano", which used to cover the street on rainy days before the street was paved.

As you walk along, look at the palaces that line the street and try to pick out the **CHURCH OF SAN GIORGIO**. It has large columns on the façade. This is is one of the most important Sienese architectural structures of the 1700s.

Turn left and at the end of the piazza you'll see the **CHURCH OF SANTO SPIRITO**. The convent of this ancient 13th century church has now

been turned into a prison. If we continue along VIA DEI PISPINI - which means *zampilli* (water jets) - we'll reach the very grand **PORTA PISPINI**, built in the first half of the 1300s. Built into the wall (☞ p. 74) to the left of the gate is one of the blockhouses built to defend Siena. In fact, it is the only one that has been preserved of all those built by the architect Baldassarre Peruzzi (☞ p. 111).

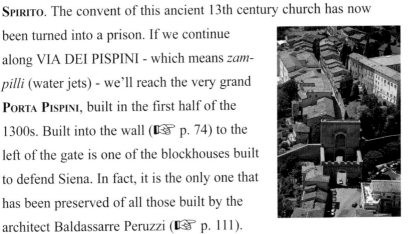

Did you know that... on via dei Pispini at n. 164 there is the ART MUSEUM FOR CHILDREN? It's a place where you can play, let your imagination run wild and learn the secrets of art.

Go back up via dei Pispini and turn onto Pantaneto near the PORTA SAN MAURIZIO, the so-called **Ponte di Romana**.

Beyond the gate turn right and walk toward the **Basilica of San Clemente in Santa Maria dei Servi**. This basilica, founded in the 13th century, is located on one of the hills that dominate the VALDIMONTONE (Valley of Montone). According to ancient legend, Romulus sent two Roman military leaders, Montonius and Camulius, to capture and bring his nephews Senius and Aschius back to Rome. The VILLAGE OF CASTELMONTORIO grew up where Montonius made camp and the valley was called, appropriately, Valdimontone.

Let's go back to Ponte di Romana and walk along via Roma. Do you see the large Renaissance palace made of tufa and with large arched windows on your left? This is **palazzo di San Galgano** and it was built at the end of the 1400s by Cistercian monks ⭐. These monks lived in the Abbey of San Galgano about 30 kilometers from Siena. I bet you'd enjoy visiting it because in a hermitage nearby there is a sword in a rock, just like King Arthur's Excalibur! In fact, on the façade of Palazzo di San Galgano you can find strange *ironware*

with the symbol of the monks - a sword stuck in a rock.

You have probably noticed strangely shaped *ironware* in many other palaces of the city. Do you know what they were used for?

Look at the drawings and put down the matching number (☞ 10 p. 122)

1) for tying up horses
2) for hanging birdcages or hanging out the washing
3) for holding banners or torches

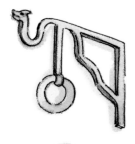

At the end of via Roma you see in front of you **PORTA ROMA-NA**, the largest of all the gates in Siena. As you already know, via Francigena (☞ p. 71) came out this gate and continued south towards Rome, which is why the gate is called "romana".

Porta Romana, like porta Pispini, still has its *barbican* (☞ p. 75). Walk through it and stop in front of the entrance arch so you can see the sun with the letters JHS. Do you remember who this symbol belonged to? And why it was placed over the doors of the houses and the gates of the city? (☞ 11 p.122)

_____

_____

_____

What is...

the via Francigena?

The **VIA FRANCIGENA** is a road of Lombard origins. In the Middle Ages
it was the most important road
connecting northern Europe to
Rome.

The via Francigena crossed Siena
when it passed through Tuscany.
Siena was a very important stop for
people continuing the journey
because after Siena there wasn't
another city where they could stay for about 140 kilometers.

The via *Francigena* entered Siena through porta Camollia, ran along
the hill of Castelvecchio and went out through porta Romana.
In the 1200s, along the part of the Francigena that crossed the city,
you could find workshops and *stands* of moneychangers for trading.

There were also many
many taverns, inns,
warehouses, stables and
hospitals, which gave
hospitality and
refreshment to passing
strangers.

What is... a pilgrim?

In addition to the merchants, knights and bandits
who travelled on the via Francigena, there were also
many PILGRIMS. These were people who wanted
to save their souls by going to Jerusalem, to Rome
or to Santiago de Compostela in Spain.
For these long journeys pilgrims needed
special clothing. Here is what was necessary for a good trip:

- a large *cloak*, called a *sarrochino*, to protect them from the cold and rain;
- a tall strong *walking stick*, called a *bordone*, to help them walk
- an empty *gourd*, tied to the end of their walking stick, to keep water in;
- a hat with a wide brim;
- a leather bag, or *bisaccia*, to hold food.

Before leaving, the pilgrim and all of his possessions were blessed.
When he returned, the pilgrim pinned a small object, a
type of *souvenir,* to his clothing to prove that he had
really completed his journey.

Whoever reached Jerusalem wore a *palm*. Those who
had been to Rome hung small squares of blessed
cloth called *pazienze* on their clothing. And whoever
arrived all the way to Santiago de Compostela hung a
shell around his neck or on
his cloak when he
returned.

What are...

the Biccherna Covers?

The **BICCHERNA COVERS** are the wodden panels used as covers of large registers where the City of Siena listed all of its expenses and its income.

They were actually paintings done by famous painters from the 13th-18th centuries. They are very important because they help us understand the customs of the city. There are 103 panels preserved to this day. The most famous painters who painted the Biccherna covers are Duccio, Sano di Pietro, Vecchietta, Francesco di Giorgio Martini and many others (☞ p. 104-111). Today you can see the collection of

these small masterpieces in the MUSEUM OF THE BICCHERNA COVERS inside the State Archives of Siena in palazzo Piccolomini.

What are... the walls?

Siena has had many city **WALLS** over the centuries. They never built the new walls around the older ones, but just added extensions.

The walls were made with mortar ⭐ and rubble ⭐ and faced with bricks and in a few places, with stone. They were six to nine meters high and about one and a half meters thick.

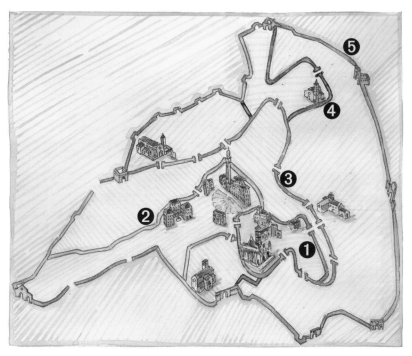

❶ The first city walls extended around Castelvecchio.

❷ New walls were made in the middle of the 13th century and included the city part of the Francigena to the north.

❸ Between 1150 and 1250 the increase in population caused the creation of new villages. The walls were enlarged to include the districts of Ovile, San Martino, Pispini, Fontebranda and Valdimontone. In this way the walls included another piece of the Francigena to the south.

❹ Under the Government of the Nine (1287-1355) two other sections of wall were begun. These enclosed the districts of the Basilica of San Francesco and those of Fontebranda and Pispini.

❺ In the 1500s Siena was defended by walls which entirely surrounded the city for seven kilometers.

From porta Pispini to San Prospero the walls alternated with large towers and had a *walkway* where soldiers made their rounds ⭐.
Some gates, like porta Pispini and porta Romana, had a *barbican*, a gate before the main one which served as a small barrack square. In times of peace it was used to collect the customs ⭐ from people who brought goods into the city. The gate itself contained the rooms for the guards, storerooms for the arms and a covered part for the mechanisms of the drawbridge.

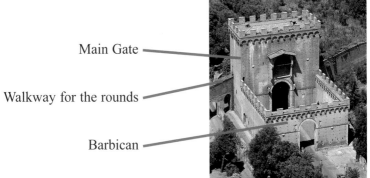

Main Gate

Walkway for the rounds

Barbican

Terzo di Camollia

This route will help you discover the most interesting places in the
Terzo di Camollia.

Do you remember the legend I told you about *Montonius* and *Camulius*, the militay leaders that Romulus sent to capture his rebel nephews Aschius and Senius? Well, the place where *Camulius* set up camp took his name, and this was later changed to **CAMOLLIA**.

Now, imagine you are a knight in the Middle Ages who is traveling the via Francigena (p. 71) and you are getting ready to enter the city through porta Camollia.

PORTA CAMOLLIA was the most strongly defended of all the gates of Siena because it had to protect the city from attacks coming from the Florentine territory. Even today it is very impressive!

In 1270 the Sienese built an outer gate, a strong high ANTIPORTO, to defend itself even better from Florence. The space between porta Camollia and the Antiporto was

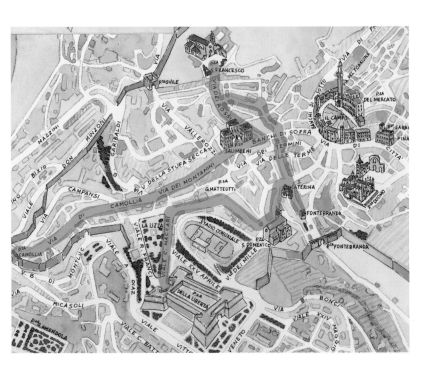

also used as a field for fairs and markets. When Ferdinando I dei Medici entered the city through porta Camollia, the Sienese placed the coat of arms of the Medici family on the entrance arch along with the following words in Latin: **COR MAGIS TIBI SENA PANDIT** which means: "Siena opens her heart to you even more (than this gate)". The Sienese of that time were forced to display this inscription. Today, however, it

is a symbol of great welcome and hospitality. If you look carefully higher up, you will find another symbol that you should recognize: the large sun with the letters "JHS". Let's enter the city and walk along VIA CAMOLLIA, an old section of the via Francigena within the city walls (☞ p. 74).

The first important monument we come to is the very old **CHURCH OF SAN PIETRO ALLA MAGIONE**. It belonged to the Order of the Knights Templar - the Templars  - who built a series of houses, the so-called Magione, around the church and a hospital to assist the pilgrims (☞ p. 72). You can still see the beautiful Gothic portal of the church (☞ p. 100).

Beyond Camollia, the old via Francigena continued with the present VIA DEI MONTANINI. The name comes from the family that had their "castellare" in this area. Continue down via Montanini and you arrive in **Piazza Salimbeni**. Here the powerful and rich Sienese

Salimbeni family saw their fortified citadel destroyed and rebuilt many times over the course of the centuries.

Originally, in place of the piazza you see today, there was only a short narrow street leading to the large door of the fortress. Then, at the end of the 19th century, the Sienese architect Giuseppe Partini (☞ p. 111)

decided to create the piazza to give prestige to the **Rocca Salimbeni**. Following the fashion of the time of building in a way that copied the original style, he rebuilt the façade in perfect Gothic style.

The buildings which surround the piazza today are the headquarters of the Monte dei Paschi Bank, one of the oldest banks in Europe.

Did you know that... near here, on via della Sapienza 5, there is the **Biblioteca Comunale degli Intronati** (City Library)? Here you can find precious manuscripts and very old books.

Continue along **via Banchi di Sopra**, which was also an old part of the via Francigena. Its name comes from the stands of the workshops and moneychangers that used to be set up along this street.

A little ahead on your left is **Arco dei Rossi**, which used to be the entrance to the castellare of the Rossi family. As you walk along via dei Rossi, notice all the beautiful noble palaces you see. At the end of the street there is a large arch that opens onto a piazza with the imposing **Basilica of San Francesco**.

At the end of the 1200s the City of Siena decided to build a church in honor of St Francis. They chose this place because it was spacious enough for the Franciscan friars to welcome the large number of the faithful who came to listen to their sermons. To build the **Basilica** ⭐ **of San Francesco** the friars also used the money that the usurers ⭐ and thieves donated so they would be pardoned for their sins.

Go inside this Gothic church. As you see, it has only one large nave ⭐ covered with a wooden trussed ⭐ ceiling and with the transept ⭐ divided into many very tall chapels. Such a large space could receive a crowd of believers.

A large part of the treasury of the church was destroyed by a terrible fire in the 1600s. Although the marbles alters were destroyed, fortunately, they managed to save part of the *frescos* (☞ p. 40) done by the brothers Pietro and Ambrogio Lorenzetti (☞ p. 108-109). If you want to admire them, go inside the chapel on the left transept. There you will see a painting of the *Crucifixion* by Pietro and the

paintings of *St Louis of Toulouse before Boniface VIII* and the *Martyrdom of the Franciscans* by Ambrogio.

In the **CHAPEL OF THE SACRAMENT** they keep the CONSECRATED

HOST. These sacred wafers have remained intact since 1730. Their story begins when some thieves stole a ciborium which contained these Hosts from the basilica.

Three days later the Hosts were found in the alms box in the Basilica of Santa Maria in Provenzano. They were brought back to the Basilica of San Francesco. The friars decided not the consume them and since that time they have been preserved intact, without mold or bacteria, despite the 270 years which have passed!

Bernardo Albizzeschi, now known as St Bernardine (☞ p. 113), became a Franciscan friar in this basilica on 8 September 1402. The Oratory located on the right side of the piazza is dedicated to him. On that spot Bernadine preached to the faithful and showed them the tablet with the sun and the letters "JHS". You might enjoy visiting it, because inside there is also the **DIOCESAN MUSEUM OF SACRED ART**, rich in precious works of art.

The clothes make the monk...

Would you be able to recognize which monk wears these clothes?

- -

FRANCISCAN: order of St Francis of Assisi
brown frock

DOMINICAN: order of St Dominic
white tunic, black cloak, white scapular

AUGUSTINIAN: order of St Augustine
black frock with scapular, leather belt

CARMELITE: order of Our Lady of Mt. Carmel
brown dress with white mantle and hood (☞ 12 p. 122)

After you leave piazza San Francesco, turn left immediately after the arch and walk along a series of streets and alleys until you reach the BASILICA OF SANTA MARIA IN PROVENZANO. In this area the Salvani family had their castellare, which was completely destroyed in 1270 by their enemies, the Tolomei family.

The basilica of Santa Maria in Provenzano was built at the end of the 1500s to house the terra-cotta image of the Madonna which had performed several miracles.
This work is very special to the people of Siena and, in fact the Palio of 2 July is run (☞ p. 92) in honor of this holy image.

Let's continue until we reach **Piazza Tolomei**.

The piazza is dominated by PALAZZO TOLOMEI, home of the noble Sienese Tolomei family. This elegant Gothic building (☞ p. 100) with its perforated bifore ⭐ windows is one of the most prestigious in all of Siena. See those holes on the ground floor?

Do you remember what they're called and what their function was? (☞ 13 p. 122)

Opposite the palace is the **CHURCH OF SAN CRISTOFORO**, one of the oldest in Siena. It was built in the Romanesque style (☞ p. 100) between the 11th and the 12th centuries, but was completely restructured in the 1800s. The Council of the Bell used to meet inside this church. If you don't remember what that was, turn to page 17.

Before we go on with our tour, you might like to see the special CASTELLARE of the **UGURGERI** family. It's quite nearby.

If you cross via dei Termini and via delle Terme and go down a steep hill, you'll come to the **BIRTHPLACE OF ST CATHERINE OF SIENA**.

Directly in front of you is the **PORTICO DEI COMUNI D'ITALIA**. Its name come from the fact that each Italian city gave enough money to buy one brick. Work on it was begun in 1939, when St Catherine (☞ p. 112) was proclaimed the Patron Saint of Italy. If you cross the arcade and go down a few steps, you'll come to the **CHURCH OF THE CRUCIFIX**. Inside the church is the 12th century *Crucifix* from which, legend says, Catherine received the stigmata ⭐ in the city of Pisa.

In front of the church is the entrance to the **KITCHEN ORATORY**. It was built over the remains of the old kitchen of Catherine's family. In fact, under the altar you can still see the blackened wall of the fireplace. The 16th century paintings which decorate the walls represent episodes from the life of the saint.

Downstairs to your right is Catherine's bedroom. In this small room Catherine loved to pray and rest.

There are a few relics  associated with the saint in a small cell: the *knob* of her walking-stick, the *lantern* she used to visit the sick at night, a *small pot* of aromas she used to ease the suffering of the sick, and the *bag* which was used to transport her head from Rome to Siena.

After visiting the Home of St Catherine, go down the steep street to your right and you'll reach **FONTEBRANDA**. This is the fountain where Catherine's father drew water to dye his cloth.

Fontebranda

This is one of the oldest and most beautiful fountains (☞ p. 90) in Siena, built between the 12th and the 13th centuries. With its

impressive lancet arches  it is typical of the Gothic style (☞ p. 100).*i*

Let's continue our journey. We return now in front of the sanctuary of Saint Catherine and, going up a steep hill, arrive at the impressive

Basilica of San Domenico

This **BASILICA** was built during the 13th century with the money of the City and that of usurers who gave great sums of money to the friars to free themselves of sins committed. Go inside. Like the basilica of San Francesco, this church also only has one large nave to receive the large number of the faithful and a wooden-trussed roof. Unfortunately, fires and earthquakes have destroyed part of the original building and many of its works of art.

On your right is the **CHAPEL OF THE VAULTS**. On the altar of the back wall you can see a fresco (☞ p. 40) from the 1300s portraying *Saint Catherine and a devotee*.

This is a unique image painted when the saint was still alive: it is a type of photograph of that time! Catherine is wearing the black and white clothing typical of the Dominicans and holds a lily, symbol of purity.

The author of the fresco is Andrea Vanni (☞ p. 111) a friend of Catherine's.

Let's go on with the visit. Ahead on the right, you find the **CHAPEL OF ST CATHERINE OF SIENA**, where the reliquary ⭐ of the saint's head is kept. The walls of the chapel were frescoed in the 1500s by important painters such as Antonio Bazzi, better known as Sodoma (☞ p. 111).

He who seeks, will find....

Search now among the precious paintings kept in the Basilica for one by Guido da Siena (☞ p. 111), a very old work going back to the 13th century. I'll give you a few hints: the Madonna is wearing a red dress and a blue cloak decorated with many golden lines and is pointing with one hand to the Baby Jesus, whom she holds on her lap. Mary is sitting on a large throne and the background is completely gold. Were you able to find it? (☞ 14 p. 122)

Leaving the Basilica, go towards the last leg of our long journey: the **FORTEZZA MEDICI** . This very large brick fortress was built on the orders of Cosimo I dei Medici in 1561. On the corners of the two bastions you can still see the large Medici coat of arms.

Guess who these coats of arms belong to:

(☞ 15 p. 122)

During the second half of the 1700s the Sienese created a grand garden near the Fortezza called the **LIZZA.** You can walk quietly there today or even rest your feet if they're a bit tired after our journey.

Did you know that.... Siena makes many sweets full of almonds and candied fruit? Have you ever heard of them? *Panforte, ricciarelli, cavallucci, copate and panpepato*, - many delicious things for the greedy person with a sweet tooth to taste!

What is... a fountain?

According to a medieval legend, a river of the purest water once flowed under the city of Siena.

The name of the river was *Diana*. For a long time the City searched for the river *Diana*, but every attempt failed. Water was found in the area around Siena, however, and it was brought into the city through underground canals.

These canals are sometimes actual tunnels, which are called **BOTTINI**. The bottini were always kept in perfect condition to transport water. Emperor Charles V, after a visit to the bottini, said that Siena was formed of two equally beautiful cities: one under ground and one above. The bottini are still used today and you can visit them.

Thanks to the bottini, Siena already had in the Middle Ages beautiful wells, cisterns and fountains.

Today the fountains are no longer used as they were at one time (remember that in the past water didn't arrive in the houses), but you can still admire their very beautiful architectural structure. Each

fountain is made up of many basins. The first fountain had canals with flowing drinkable water. It was the most beautiful and had the biggest basin and was always covered with a parapet ⭐ that allowed only people who went to draw water to enter. The second basin was the WATERING TROUGH of the domestic animals and was filled with the *overflow* of the first basin. The third basin was used as a WASHING-TROUGH. From here the waste water went into the watering-place and was used by the dye-works and the tannery. A part of this waste water was finally channeled to the mills.

The City paid guards to watch over the fountains. Anyone who did not respect the laws and threw garbage into the basins was punished.

Having fountains and cisterns in the City also allowed people to react quickly if there was a fire. Unfortunately, this happened very often in the Middle Ages.

by Luca Betti

he Palio of Siena is not a simple horse race! It is a Festival of the whole city.

The Palio is run on the 2nd of July and the 16th of August each year, but in particular circumstances special palios may be run. The ring of the Piazza del Campo is covered with a layer of special earth called tufa sand ⭐. Bleachers are set up all around the piazza and the inside of the piazza is fenced off.

The origins: in the Middle Ages the Sienese festivals were jousts, tournaments and matches, bull hunts, cattle races, and races through the streets of the city on unmounted horses. Only in the 1600s did the Palio assume the aspect it has today: a horse race with a jockey in the Piazza del Campo.

The Contrade: the city is subdivided into seventeen Contrade, which are like small cities within the mother city. The contrade have picturesque names of real or mythological animals. Some are rivals of each other and on the days of the Palio there might be a few quarrels and small "skirmishes". The Contrade can also have special

The Contrade

Aquila
(Eagle)

Bruco
(Caterpillar)

Chiocciola
(Snail)

Civetta
(Owl)

Drago
(Dragon

Giraffa
(Giraffe)

Istrice
(Porcupine)

Leocorno
(Unicorn)

Lupa
(She-wolf)

Nicchio
(Shell)

Oca
(Goose)

Onda
(Wave)

Pantera
(Panther)

Selva
(Forest)

Tartuca
(Tortoise)

Torre
(Tower)

Valdimontone
(Ram)

relationships with others who become their *allies*.

Each Contrada has its own "government" elected by all of the members of the contrada. They include: the *prior*, the absolute head; the *captain*, who takes care of relationships with the jockey and the other Contrade during the days of the Palio; and two *lieutenants* or *mangini*, who help the captain.

During the year each Contrada celebrates is own titular saint. They honor their *protectors* and their sister Contradas by going around the city with the Contrada members all dressed up and carrying their flags and drums.

The young Contrada members have their own organization within the Contrada and prepare games and parties. Even the "little ones" have a special place reserved for them in the bleachers or terraces for the Palio.

The horse: is also called "*barbero*" and he is the true protagonist of the Palio. He is assigned to the Contrada by a drawing of lots and can not be substituted for any reason. In the days of the Palio he is watched over, taken care of, loved and coddled. And he lives in a comfortable stable, or often even a proper house, within the Contrada itself. Before the race he is taken to the Contrada church and blessed by the *correttore*, or the priest, with the words "go and return the victor".

The jockey: is a true professional who is hired and paid by the

Contrada to run and try to win the Palio. He is also expected to make the enemy Contrada lose.

The Drappellone: also known as the "Palio", is a large painted silk cloth which is the prize for the winner. Often is painted by internationally famous painters.

The Historic Procession: takes place before the race. When the "Big Bell" rings, the costumed participants from the Contrade and the City file into Piazza del Campo. The

procession ends with the "carroccio", a war cart pulled by oxen, which carries the prize for the winner: the drappellone, or Palio.

The extraction by lots:

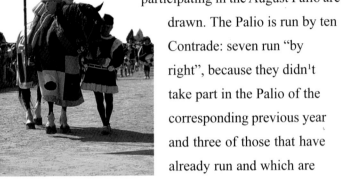

On the last Sunday in May the Contrade which will take part in the July Palio are drawn by lots, while on the first Sunday in July those participating in the August Palio are drawn. The Palio is run by ten Contrade: seven run "by right", because they didn¹t take part in the Palio of the corresponding previous year and three of those that have already run and which are drawn by lots to participate in the race.

Assigning of the horses: On 29 June and 13 August the horses are presented and selected by veterinarians. They are divided into heats and run in the Piazza. The Mayor then draws lots and assigns the ten horses chosen for the Palio.

The trials: There are six trials and they take place in the early morning and late afternoon on the days before the Palio. It is not important who wins the trials; they serve only to judge the condition of the horse and the jockey. After the trial on the evening before the Palio, each Contrada organizes a propitiatory dinner called the *dinner of the General Trial*. Hundreds of people come to eat at the tables set up in the quarters throughout the city.

The race:

The horses with their jockeys come out of the courtyard of the Palazzo Pubblico, which is called the "entrone". At the order of the *starter*, they line up at the *canape*, two large taut hemp ropes. The horse of the last Contrada stays outside the ropes and then throws himself in at a *running start*. At that point the starter orders the lowering of the rope and then the *mossa* (move) or, the starting. The jockeys wear a jacket and a metallic helmet (the so-called zucchino) in the colors of the Contrada. It's not

always easy to stay on the back of the horse because the Palio is run bareback, without a saddle!

When the jockeys leave the entrone they receive a small whip called a *nerbo*, with which they can spur on their own horse. They also use it to disturb the jockeys of the other Contrade. The horses must complete three turns around the Piazza (almost a kilometer run in little more than a minute). The finish-line is a few meters from the starting-line and is indicated by a small black and white flag. The drum and the explosion of a *firecracker* welcome the winning horse and indicate the end of the race. An unmounted horse, one without a jockey, can also win.

The celebrations:

The victorious jockey and horse are brought back in triumph to the Basilica di Santa Maria in Provenzano (for the July Palio) or to the Duomo (for the August Palio).

The Contrada members parade through the streets in the middle of the rejoicing crowd. Celebrations continue the whole night long. In the following weeks the Contrada will continue to celebrate their victory with dinners and celebrations in the streets of their district. They also celebrate with the *victory dinner* at end of

September. Everyone waits for this final party and there might be as many as three or four thousand people sitting down to dinner in the streets of the Contrada. One very special place is set for the star of the evening, the victorious horse, and he is placed at ... the head table!

Did you know that...

each Contrada has its own **Museum** where they jealously keep all the Palios they have won?

The styles

Over the centuries artists have worked following the "fashion" of their times. This fashion in art is called style. Each style applies to painting, sculpture and architecture. Now I'll help you recognize the most important styles.

Romanesque Style

The Romanesque style developed throughout Europe in 1000 and continued through the 1100s. Public and religious buildings were built following this new style and typically have massive walls and strong columns. The façades are decorated with stones, colored marble, golden mosaics and marble inlays (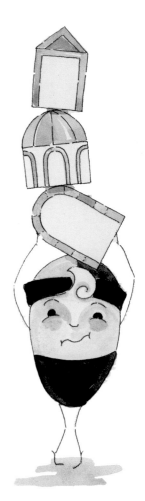 p. 61). The windows have round arches. In Siena there are no important buildings left which were built in the Romanesque style!

Gothic Style

The word "gothic" once was used with contempt because the Goths were a barbarian people. It indicates the art found in the period from the end of the 1100s to the first half of the 1300s. The Gothic style was born in northern France near Paris and spread throughout Europe. In this period many grand cathedrals  were built, some up to 40 meters high. They usually have lancet, or pointed, arches and rampant arches, which are arches that lean against the walls. These arches reduced of the weight of the walls and allowed lightweight very colorful stained-glass windows to be placed in the large walls. The palaces were also built in the Gothic style, using both bifore and trifore lancet windows. Most of the buildings in Siena are built in this style.

The Sienese School

Between the 1200s and the 1400s the way the Sienese artists painted was very elegant and colorful, and very different from the more severe style of the Florentines. Among the most important painters were Duccio di Buoninsegna, Simone Martini, Pietro and Ambrogio Lorenzetti, and Sassetta.

Renaissance Style

The Renaissance, which developed between the 1400s and the 1500s, means "rebirth". During these years, in fact, artists gave new birth to the ancient Greek and Roman models of beauty and grace. They built buildings whose interior and exterior space was regularly divided by repetition of the same forms. In this way they produced a sense of harmony, perfection and beauty. The dominant colors are the white of

the walls, and the grey of the stone which edged the windows, doors and the round arches ⭐.

The Renaissance was a period of great artists like Brunelleschi, Donatello, Botticelli, Leonardo da Vinci, Michelangelo, Raphael, and many others.

In Siena the Logge del Papa is one of the few examples of Renaissance architecture.

Baroque Style

Baroque is an artistic period going from the end of the 1500s to the middle of the 1700s. In the Baroque style the rules are no longer respected and everything is done according to the whim of the artist. In the palaces and churches enormous frescos seem to burst through the ceiling. The altars and the walls are decorated with

large curls of gilded plaster. Cities were beautified with squares and fountains full of columns and statues. In Italy the most important city of the Baroque style is Rome, where the popes indulged their whims by having artists create grandiose works of art.

The Chapel of Our Lady of Votive offerings inside the Cathedral in Siena was built in the Baroque style.

I'd like to tell you about the life of some of the most important artists who worked in Siena

Duccio di Buoninsegna

FIRST NAME: Duccio

LAST NAME: Buoninsegna

PLACE AND DATE OF BIRTH AND DEATH: Siena, 1260
Siena, 1318

PROFESSION: Painter

Duccio is the first great Sienese painter. Art historians think that as a young man he was a friend of Cimabue and maybe worked in his workshop in Florence. He painted some of the Biccherna covers (☞ p. 73), but his specialty was paintings of the Madonna. In 1311 Duccio finished his magnificent *Maestà* ⭐ and the Sienese had a solemn procession to take

the enormous painting from the painter's workshop to the Cathedral. Today it is kept in the Museo dell'Opera. Inside the Cathedral Duccio also made the very colorful round stained-glass window (☞ p.62) in the center of the apse. Duccio di Buoninsegna is important because his painting is more modern than that of his contemporaries. The scenes in his paintings are full of characters and the colors are brilliant. The Madonnas have sweet faces and soft clothing, and are surrounded with a great light because Duccio used a lot of gold in the background.

Simone Martini

First Name: Simone

Last Name: Martini

Place and Date of Birth and Death:

Siena, 1284 - Avignone, 1344

Profession: Painter

Simone is one of the most famous artists of Sienese painting of the 1300s. As a young man he admired the work of Duccio di Buoninsegna and perhaps worked in his workshop. In 1315 the City of Siena asked Simone to fresco (☞ p. 40) a large *Maestà* in the Palazzo Pubblico. It was so beautiful that some years later the City had him also fresco the opposite wall with the portrait of the knight *Guidoriccio da Fogliano*. The artist became so famous that even the pope wanted him to work in his court in Avignone. Simone

Martini is a very refined painter. His characters seem to come from an enchanted world. The Madonnas are as elegant as Ladies and the saints are like knights. To make his works more precious, Simone also used gold leaf, colorful semiprecious stones and parchment.

Nicola Pisano

FIRST NAME: Nicola

LAST NAME: Unknown, called Pisano because he worked in Pisa

PLACE AND DATE OF BIRTH AND DEATH:

Puglia, 1210/1215 - 1278/1284

PROFESSION: Sculptor and Architect

Nicola, a native from Puglia, moved to Pisa when he was very young. There, in 1260, he sculpted the very beautiful marble *Pulpit* for the Baptistry. A short time later he arrived in Siena with his son Giovanni and made the *Pulpit* in the Cathedral. Once he was famous, he was asked to work in many cities, like Pistoia, Lucca and Perugia, where he sculpted the large Fountain. Nicola Pisano was inspired in his

works by Greek and Roman statues, but he did not copy them. On the contrary, his works are considered more alive and expressive.

Giovanni Pisano

FIRST NAME: Giovanni

LAST NAME: Unknown, called Pisano

PLACE AND DATE OF BIRTH AND DEATH:
Pisa, 1240/1245 - Siena, after 1314

PROFESSION: Sculptor and Architect

Giovanni learned his craft as a sculptor from his father Nicola and he worked with him on the *Pulpit* in Siena and on the *Fountain* in Perugia. After the death of his father he became the master "builder" of the Cathedral of Siena. He planned the Cathedral *Façade* and sculpted some of the statues for its decoration. Today these works are in the Museo dell'Opera. Following a dispute with the City, Giovanni suddenly left Siena and moved to Pisa, where he directed the works for the Cathedral.

At the same time he sculpted the *Pulpit* for the Church of Sant'Andrea in Pistoia and the one for the Cathedral of Pisa.

The style of Giovanni Pisano is different from that of his father. His characters are energetic and wide-awake and turn in a spiral.

Pietro Lorenzetti

FIRST NAME: Pietro

LAST NAME: Lorenzetti

PLACE AND DATE OF BIRTH AND DEATH: Siena, 1280 - Siena, 1348 during the plague

SPECIAL NOTES: older brother of Ambrogio

PROFESSION: Painter

As a young man, Pietro learned his craft as a painter in Siena from the students of Duccio di Buoninsegna. He was so good that he was immediately asked to come to other cities. He painted masterpieces in Assisi, Arezzo and Florence. When he returned to Siena, he became the official painter of the City. He worked along with his brother Ambrogio on the large fresco (☞ p. 40) on the façade of the Spedale di Santa Maria della Scala, which is no longer present today, and in the convent of San Francesco.

The painting of Pietro Lorenzetti was inspired by that of Giotto. The characters, animals and palaces of his paintings are similar to the real ones.

Ambrogio Lorenzetti

FIRST NAME: Ambrogio

LAST NAME: Lorenzetti

PLACE AND DATE OF BIRTH AND DEATH:

Siena, 1285 - Siena, 1348 during the plague

SPECIAL NOTES: younger brother of Pietro

PROFESSION: Painter

Ambrogio worked a lot in Florence and when he returned to Siena, he did the large frescos (☞ p. 40), *Allegory of the Good and Bad Government* and its *Effects on the City and the Countryside,* in the Palazzo Pubblico.

Together with his brother, he worked on the lost frescos on the facade

of the Spedale di Santa Maria della Scala and on those of the convent of San Francesco. The works of Ambrogio Lorenzetti are so true and rich in details that they help us understand how people lived in Siena in the 1300s.

Jacopo della Quercia

FIRST NAME: Jacopo

LAST NAME: di Pietro d'Angelo, called "della Quercia" because he was born in the village of Quercegrossa, near Siena

PLACE AND DATE OF BIRTH AND DEATH:

Quercegrossa (Si), 1371 - Siena, 1438

PROFESSION: Sculptor

Jacopo was the son of a goldsmith and he began to work when he was very young. He immediately showed a great talent.

He had a restless character and often fought with his patrons.
This also happened when he was working on the *Gaia Fountain* in Piazza del Campo.

Due to his disorderly life he was frequently reported to the authorities. Despite this, the sculptures of Jacopo were so beautiful that many cities wanted to beautify their cathedrals and piazzas with his works. He worked in Siena, Florence, Bologna and in Lucca, where he sculpted the wonderful *Tomb of Ilaria del Caretto*.

The elegant and harmonious style of Jacopo della Quercia was studied also by the young Michelangelo.

and...

Arnolfo di Cambio
sculptor, architect (Colle Val d'Elsa, Siena, 1245 - Florence, 1302)
Domenico Beccafumi
painter (Siena, 1486 -1551)
Michelangelo Buonarroti
painter, sculptor, architect (Caprese, Arrezzo, 1475 - Rome, 1564)
Domenico di Bartolo
painter (Asciano, Siena - noted from 1428 to 1447)
Donatello
sculptor (Florence, 1386 -1466)
Antonio Federighi
architect, sculptor (Siena, 1490 -?)
Guido da Siena
painter (active in the XIII century)
Rutilio Manetti
painter (Siena, 1571 - 1639)
Francesco di Giorgio Martini
architect, sculptor, painter, military engineer ((Siena, 1439 -1502)
Baldassarre Peruzzi
painter, architect (Siena, 1481 - Rome 1536)
Giuseppe Partini
architect (Siena, 1842 - 1895)
Pinturicchio
painter (Perugia, 1554 - Siena, 1513)
Sano di Pietro
painter (Siena, 1406 - 1481)
Tito Sarrocchi
sculptor (Siena, 1824 - 1900)
Sodoma (Antonio Bazzi, called Sodoma)
painter (Vercelli, 1477 - Siena, 1549)
Spinello Aretino
painter (Arezzo, 1350 - 1410)
Andrea Vanni
painter (Siena, 1332 - 1414)
Vecchietta
painter, sculptor (Castiglion d'Orcia, Siena, 1412 - Siena, 1480)

The "Sienese" Saints

Saint Catherine of Siena

Catherine Benincase was born in Siena in 1347. She was the next to last of 25 brothers and sisters. At the age of 12 she was a very beautiful girl but she refused the marriage desired by her parents because she wanted to enter the order of the sisters of San Domenico. She dedicated herself immediately to charity and many important people were attracted by her faith. Catherine traveled throughout all of Italy. Even though she didn't know how to write, she dictated letters and sent them to powerful men like kings and queens and popes to obtain peace among peoples. She received the stigmata in Pisa in 1375. She died in Rome on 29 April 1380 when she was only 33. Her body is preserved in Rome in the Church of Santa Maria Sopra Minerva, but her head is in Siena in the Basilica of San Domenico.

St Catherine of Siena is the Patron Saint of Italy and of Europe.

How to recognize her in paintings

She is a saint with a white dress and veil and a black mantle. She has stigmata and holds a crucifix. She may also have a crown of thorns, a lily, or a book.

Saint Bernardine

Bernardine was born in Massa Marittima into the noble Albizzeschi family in 1380. When he was only 6, he became an orphan and went to live with his aunt and uncle in Siena. He studied law there as a young man. During an epidemic of the plague, he dedicated himself to healing the sick and on 8 September 1402 he became a friar in the Basilica of San Francesco. He began to preach and travelled from city to city. During his sermons he showed people a tablet with the symbol of the name of Jesus: a sun with the letters "JHS" (Jesus, Saviour of Men) in the center, and invited the faithful to kneel before it. His sermons in the Piazza del Campo and in Piazza San Francesco are famous. While preaching in the city of L'Aquila, he was taken with fever and died. He was declared Saint in 1450, only four years after his death.

How to recognize him in paintings

St Bernadine is always represented as a very thin old man, dressed in the brown frock of the Franciscans and holding a tablet with the sun and the letters "JHS".

Saint Ansanus

Ansanus was the son of a noble Roman senator. When he was 12 he converted to Christianity and began his preaching. His father reported him to the emperor Diocletian, but Ansanus managed to escape and reached Siena. There he was arrested and imprisoned in a tower in Castelvecchio. From a small window Ansanus continued to preach and to baptize the Sienese. The pagans decided then to kill him and prepared a large cauldron of boiling oil. But as soon as Ansanus was put into the cauldron, the oil stopped boiling. Although he survived this martyrdom, they then decided to cut off his head. His falling head bounced three times, and where it landed the earth gushed with water. His body is in the Cathedral of Siena, but his head is in Arezzo. The Sienese celebrate him on the 1st of December.

How to recognize him in paintings

He is a young man with a helmet of blond hair. He is dressed as a Roman soldier and has a flag - a black and white banner - and a palm, the symbol of his martyrdom. Often he is pictured baptizing people, since he was the person who converted the Sienese to Christianity.

Saint Victor

Victor preached Christianity in Egypt and was decapitated by the judge Sebastian between 14 - 15 May 178 A.D. His remains are kept in the Cathedral of Siena and in that of Volterra.

How to recognize him in paintings

He is portrayed as a young warrior with a dark brown beard. He may be holding a thin red cross, a sword or an olive branch.

Saint Sabinus

Sabinus was a bishop of Faenza. On 30 October 300 A.D. he was whipped to death. His remains are kept in the Cathedral of Siena.

How to recognize him in paintings

He is represented as an old bishop with a short beard.

Saint Crescentius

Crescentius preached Christianity and for this reason, he was decapitated in Rome somewhere along the via Salaria in 396 A.D. His remains are kept in the Cathedral of Siena.

How to recognize him in paintings

He is pictured as a young warrior with a sword, or else as decapitated.

ALLEGORY: painting, sculpture, or poetry which describes a thought by means of symbols. The allegory was much used by the artists of the Middle Ages and the Renaissance and took its inspiration from human life, the seasons, and the vices and virtues.

APSE: semicircular structure, generally found at the end of the nave of a church, but it may also be found in the side aisles or in the transept.

BAPTISMAL FONT: basin containing the water for baptism.

BAPTISTRY: religious building where people were baptized.

BASILICA: large church in the form of a rectangle with an apse, divided into a nave and two or more aisles.

BIFORE: Window with two openings divided by a small column.

BURNISHER: instrument made up of a small wooden handle on which was set a stone of agate or the very smooth tooth of a carnivorous animal. The burnisher was used to polish the golden background of a painting.

CANON: priest who lives on the Cathedral premises.

CARROCCIO: low heavy cart pulled by oxen during battle. On the cart there was a bell and two very tall poles called *pales*, from which flew the standard of the city and a sacred image.

CATHEDRAL: Christian church which housed the *cathedra* (large throne) of the bishop.

CENTAUR: fantasy character with the chest and head of a man and the body and four legs of a horse.

CIBORIUM: The bowl that contains the consecrated eucharistic Host prepared for Holy Communion.

CISTERCIAN: monk belonging to an order founded in 1098 in Citeaux, France.

COFFERED CEILING: ceiling formed of large painted or gilded wodden squares.

COIN: to make money.

CONSISTORY: a council or church governing body.

DUTY: tax to be paid on goods entering the city.

FASCISM: historical period between 1922 and 1945 during which Italy was governed by the dictatorship of Benito Mussolini.

FRAUD: deception.

FURY: rage, great anger.

GHETTO: city quarter set apart for the Jews.

GOLD-BEATER: artisan who, beating on an anvil a small layer of gold, spreads it and reduces it to a very thin sheet.

LANCET ARCH: pointed arch.

MAESTÀ: image of the Virgin with Child enthroned like a queen, surrounded by saints and angels.

MAGNANIMITY: generosity.

MERLON: solid intervals between the indentations of a battlement.

MORTAR: mixture of gravel and lime used to hold bricks together.

NAVE: space inside the church divided by columns and pillars. The central nave is more spacious and higher than the side aisles.

NICHE: a recess in the wall that serves to hold a statue or a decoration.

PARAPET: protection placed on the edges of bridges, terraces, windows, and fountains which permitted people to lean out without falling.

PATRON: the customer, or whoever orders and pays for work - a painting, a fresco or something else.

PINACOTECA: museum containing only paintings.

PORTAL: large external door of a church.

PREDELLA: painted platform under the base of a picture.

PROPHET: wise person who predicts the future, and who is chosen by God to bring his word to all people.

PUNCH: instrument with a shaped point used to imprint marks and decorations on a golden surface of a painting.

RELIC: object or part of the body of Jesus, Mary or a saint.

RISORGIMENTO: historical period between the XVIII and XIX century during which Italy fought for liberty and unity.

ROUND ARCH: an arch forming a perfect semicircle.

ROUNDS: turn patrol along the defensive walls of the city.

RUBBLE: fragments of stone.

SIBYL: woman who predicted the future in the ancient world.

SIENESE ARCH: a lancet arch with another arch a bit below it.

SINOPIA: drawing to make a fresco done with a special ochre red powder. This colored powder owes its name to the ancient city of *Sinope* on the Black Sea. If a fresco is ruined, we can know what it was like by looking at its sinopia left on the wall.

SPEDALE: hospital.

SPIRE: the pointed top of a bell tower or a painted panel. It can have the form of a triangle or pyramid.

STIGMATA: wounds of Christ (feet, hands and side) present on the body of some saints.

SYNAGOGUE: place where the Jews met to read the holy scriptures and pray.

TABERNACLE: an ornamental container or shelter for holy objects.

TEMPERANCE: patience.

TEMPLAR: "Knight of the temple" that defended the Holy Tomb in Jerusalem.

TYMPANUM (GABLE): triangular part placed at the summit of the facade of a church.

TRANSEPT: short arm of the cross in the layout of a church.

TRECCOLONE: seller of eggs, chickens and rabbits.

TRIFORE: window with three openings in the form of an arch divided by two small columns.

TRUSS: structure with wooden beams to support the roof.

TUFA SAND: sand or porous rock made from volcanic deposits.

USURER: person who lends money, requiring for it a repayment with large profit.

VIA AURELIA: Roman consular road which ran along the Tyrrhenian coast.

VIA CASSIA: Roman consular road which ran along the Apennines.

VOTIVE LAMP: light placed in front of a sacred image and kept lit out of devotion.

...and now I will draw Siena

Solutions

1. On the back wall

2. From the Balzana located over the tents in the encampment

3. The intruder is the ladybug

4. It represents the common good and, by allegory, the City of Siena

5. Temperance, Prudence, Discord, Cruelty

6. From the top to the bottom:

   1) Pulpit

   2) Our Lady of the Vow

   3) Wheel of Fortune

7. The correct answer is C.

8. The battle of Montaperti was won by the Sienese.

9. The saint with the banner is St Ansanus.

10. The solution is: 3, 1, 2.

11. St Bernadine, to ask protection from Jesus

12. The right order is: Franciscan, Carmelite, Augustinian, Dominican

13. They are called pontaie holes and they are used to insert poles which supported scaffolding or a projecting balcony.

14. The painting of Guido da Siena is found in the transept, in the second chapel to the left of the altar.

15. The correct order is: Medici, City of Siena (Balzana), Santa Maria della Scala, Opera del Duomo.

Useful Numbers

Churches, Museums, Places to visit

Accademia Chigiana (Palazzo Chigi Saracini)
via di Città, 89 - tel. 0577 22091 - www.chigiana.it

Basilica di S. Clemente in Santa Maria dei Servi
piazza Manzoni - tel. 0577 223420
Free entrance

Basilica di San Domenico
piazza San Domenico - tel. 0577 280893
Free entrance

Basilica di San Francesco
piazza San Francesco - tel. 0577 289081
Free entrance

Basilica di Santa Maria in Provenzano
piazza Provenzano Salvani - tel. 0577 285253
Free entrance

Baptistry of San Giovanni
piazza San Giovanni - tel. 0577 283048
Entrance free to children under 11

Biblioteca Communale degli Intronati (City Library)

via della Sapienza, 5 - tel. 0577 280704

Free entrance - www.biblioteca.comune.siena.it

Botanical Garden

via Pier Andrea Mattioli, 4 - tel. 0577 232874

Free entrance

Bottini of Siena

La Diana Association - tel. 0577 41110

www.comune.siena.it/diana

Church of Sant'Agostino

Prato di Sant'Agostino - tel. 0577 226785 - www.sienaviva.it

Entrance free to children under 11

Civic Museum (in Palazzo Pubblico)

Piazza del Campo - tel. 0577 292226

Entrance free to children under 11

www.comune.siena.it/museocivico

Duomo (Cathedral)

piazza Duomo - tel. 0577 283048

Free entrance - www.operaduomo.siena.it

Libreria Piccolomini (in Duomo)

Entrance free to children under 11

tel. 0577 283048 - www.operaduomo.siena.it

Museum of Art for Children

via dei Pispini, 164 - tel 0577 46517

www.comune.siena.it

Museum of the Biccherna Covers (in the State Archives)

via Banchi di Sotto, 52 - tel. 0577 227145

Museo dell'Opera (Cathedral Museum)

piazza Duomo, 1 - tel. 0577 283048

Entrance free to children under 11

Museums of the Contrade

The museums are run directly by those appointed from within the Contrada itself; visits generally are possible only by reservation.

Aquila - Casato di Sotto, 82 - tel. 0577 288086
Bruco - via del Comune, 30 - tel. 0577 44842
Chiocciola - via San Marco, 37 - tel. 0577 45455
Civetta - piazza del Castellare - tel. 0577 285505
Drago - piazza Matteotti, 19 - tel. 0577 40575
Giraffa - via delle Vergini, 18 - tel. 0577 287091
Istrice - via Camollia, 89 - tel. 0577 48495
Leocorno - piazzetta Grassi, - tel. 0577 49298
Lupa - via Vallerozzi, 71/73 - tel. 0577 286038
Nicchio - via dell'Oliviera, 47 - tel. 0577 49600
Oca - vicolo del Tiratoio, 11 - tel. 0577 285413
Onda - via Giovanni Duprè, 111 - tel. 0577 48384
Pantera - via San Quirico, 26 - tel. 0577 48468
Selva - piazzetta della Selva, 4 - tel. 0577 43830
Tartuca - via Tommaso Pendola, 28 - tel. 0577 49448
Torre - via Salicotto, 80 - tel. 0577 222181
Valdimontone - via di Valdimontone, 6 - tel. 0577 222590

Museum of Natural History - Academy of Fisiocritici

Prato di Sant'Agostino, 5 - tel. 0577 47002 -

www.accademiafisiocritici.it

Free entrance

Oratorio di San Bernadino and Diocesan Museum of Sacred Art

piazza San Francesco - tel. 0577 283048

Entrance free to children under 11

Palazzo delle Papesse (Center of Contemporary Art)

via di Città, 126 - tel. 0577 220720

Entrance free to children under 11

www.papesse.org

Piccolomini Library (in the Cathedral)

Entrance free to children under 11

Pinacoteca Nazionale (National Picture Gallery)

via San Pietro, 29 - tel. 0577 281161

Entrance free to minors under 18

Sanctuary and Home of Saint Catherine

Costa Sant'Antonio, 6 - tel. 0577 288175

free entrance - www.caterinati.org

Santa Maria della Scala

piazza Duomo, 2 - tel. 0577 224811

Entrance free to children under 11

www.santamaria.comune.siena.it

Synagogue

via delle Scotte, 14 - tel. 055 2346654

www.iol.it/sinagoga

Torre del Mangia

Piazza del Campo - tel. 0577 292263

Free entrance to children under 11

www.comune.siena.it

Other useful numbers

A.P.T. (Ufficio informazioni turistiche)

Piazza del Campo, 56 - tel. 0577 280551

infoaptsiena@terrasiena.it

Auto Assistance (ACI) - 116

Bus service - 0577 204246

Customs office - 117

Fire department - 115

First Aid/ Emergency service - 0577 585689

Health Emergency - 118

Police (local) - 113 - 0577 288561

Police (National) - Carabinieri - 112

Police Headquarters of Siena - 0577 201111

Taxi - 0577-49222

Train information - Toll-free - 1478 88088

The publisher and authors gratefully acknowledge:
Superintendent Bruno Santi,
The City of Siena, the Departments of Culture and Tourism of Siena,
The Office of Tourism of Siena, Laura Bonelli, Gabriele Fattorini,
The Siena Viva Cooperative

Special thanks to Anna Bandinelli,
Roberto Cacciatori, Giuliano Catoni, Susan Scott
for their generous availability and valuable suggestions.
Translated by Jo Ann Warren.

© Betti editrice, 2001/2003 - Tutti i diritti riservati - All rights reserved
IIa edizione - Finito di stampare nel mese di marzo 2003

Betti Editrice - Betti srl - Siena
Tel & Fax 0577-298447 - mail: info@betti.it
www.betti.it